SIMPLIFY
&
CELEBRATE

Alternatives'

SIMPLIFY
&
CELEBRATE

Embracing the Soul
of Christmas

Northstone

Editors: Michael Schwartzentruber

and Kathy Sinclair

Cover and interior design: Margaret Kyle

Cover cross-stich: Julie Bachewich

Cover nativity applique : Crystal Przybille

Back cover photos: Michael Schwartzentruber

and James Taylor

Children's pages artwork: Crystal Przybille

Consulting art director: Robert MacDonald

Canadian Cataloguing in Publication Data

Main entry under title:

Simplify and celebrate

ISBN 1-896836-14-3

1. Christmas. 2. Christian life.

BV45.S55 1997   263.'91   C97-910512-9

Scripture quotes from New Revised Standard Version and An Inclusive Language Lectionary.

Northstone Publishing Inc. is an employee-owned company, committed to caring for the environment and all creation. Northstone recycles, reuses and composts, and encourages readers to do the same. Resources are printed on recycled paper and more environmentally friendly groundwood papers (newsprint), whenever possible. The trees used are replaced through donations to the Scoutrees For Canada Program. Ten percent of all profit is donated to charitable organizations.

Published by Northstone Publishing Inc, Kelowna, British Columbia

Printing 9 8 7 6 5 4 3 2 1

Printed in Canada by Transcontinental Printing Inc.

Printed on recycled paper

Contents

PART 2 : Celebrate

Advent/Christmas Calendar 1997 (C)

Traveling to Bethlehem 87

Advent/Christmas Calendar 1998 (A)

Reflections on the Gospel Texts

Advent/Christmas Calendar 1999 (B)

Christmas Reflections

About Alternatives

Resources for responsible living and celebrating since 1973

Alternatives for Simple Living – generally known as Alternatives – is a nonprofit organization whose mission is to "equip people of faith to challenge consumerism, live justly, and celebrate responsibly." Started in 1973 as a protest against the commercialization of Christmas, it encourages celebrations year-round that reflect conscientious ways of living.

Throughout its 24-year history, Alternatives has led the simple living movement. Staff and volunteers have developed a wide variety of resources, organized an annual Christmas campaign, held the Best and Worst Christmas Gift contest, led numerous workshops, and reached countless people with the message of simple, responsible living. Their emphasis is on relationships and traditions over things, aiming to avoid stress and debt, and promoting alternative giving – helping the truly needy instead of spending so much on ourselves.

Between 1973 and 1987, Alternatives published six editions of the *Alternative Celebrations Catalog*. The book *Treasury of Celebrations* (Northstone 1996) is a compendium of the best of these catalogs.

Over the years, Alternatives has also produced a quarterly magazine and three videos. The most recent video, *Break Forth into Joy!: Beyond a Consumer Lifestyle*, won a gold medal at the Houston International Film Festival (religion and ethics division).

Alternatives' most popular resource is *Whose Birthday Is It, Anyway?* This Christmas booklet for families and small groups, published since 1988, is now available in some 25 different versions for various denominations. All new each year, it contains a daily Advent calendar, biblical reflections for Advent and Christmas, activities, and a variety of other articles.

Alternatives' current list of resources includes not only material produced by Alternatives, but also books and resources from other publishers on simple living and related subjects such as hunger, the environment, and media literacy. They provide resources for Advent and Christmas, Lent and Easter, weddings, and other celebrations (some in Spanish) for adults and children.

Alternatives is funded by grants, donations, memberships, and sales of resources. The regular business line is 712-274-8875; or, call anytime to order or query membership at 1-800-821-6153. Our fax number is 1-712-274-1402. The new address is 3617 Old Lakeport Road, PO Box 2857, Sioux City, Iowa 51106. Visit their web page at http://members.aol.com/AltSimLiv/simple.html/.

Introduction

Some folks equate celebrating with elaborate and expensive events. Or, they may think of "simplifying" as a cheerless exercise.

But simplifying and celebrating really *do* go together, especially at Christmas. This book will help you simplify *and* celebrate, throughout the Christmas season. It will help you prepare for Christmas with creative ideas for simple and meaningful gift-giving, entertaining, reflecting and celebrating – with emphasis on relationships rather than stuff.

Part One contains ideas about how to simplify your Christmas – how to turn a stressful, commercialized Christmas celebration into a peaceful, meaningful one. Part Two gives readings and activities for reflection on the significance of the season. Virtually all of these resources can be used by individuals, with families, and with faith or community groups. Additional copies of specific resources in this book are available from Alternatives, 1-800-821-6153.

The present staff and Board of Director of Alternatives for Simple Living gratefully acknowledge the many previous employees and volunteers who have made this volume possible.

Gerald Iversen, National Coordinator, Alternatives for Simple Living.

PART 1

Simplify

A Simple Christmas: Getting Started

What Makes a Perfect Christmas?

What makes a "perfect" Christmas? Our responses could be anything from family togetherness to snow on Christmas Eve, from cutting back on Christmas expenses to finding a few moments of peace and solitude. Perhaps we are not even sure what would make Christmas "perfect."

But most of us can agree, Christmas is often less than perfect. There is too much shopping and wrapping, too much baking and cooking, too much party-going and entertaining. By the time the season is over, we are often physically, emotionally and financially exhausted.

Just what goes wrong? How can we experience the peace, joy and hope promised by the birth of Jesus?

Many different feelings and expectations influence the way we approach the Christmas season. One is past Christmases, and family traditions. We remember cherished childhood memories, and believe it just wouldn't be Christmas without those special thumbprint cookies, homemade dinner rolls or embroidered stockings. We remember family outings to cut a tree and fun-filled gatherings of our extended families. We remember joyous caroling and moments of peaceful reflection. We remember the sights, sounds, smells and tastes of Christmases past.

In addition to our childhood memories, we are bombarded by advertisements and seasonal articles that tell us how to make Christmas perfect. You've seen the magazines with pages and pages of decadent desserts, and the TV commercials for the latest electronic toys and kitchen gadgets. And don't forget the pressure we might feel from our family, friends and neighbors – to hang twinkling lights on our eaves and to set up a flashing Santa in our yards, to buy our children mountains of gifts so they can compare notes with the Jones' kids, to send Christmas cards to an ever-increasing list of people.

The demands seem never-ending. Each year, Christmas becomes a time to check items off "to-do" lists and to fill in the dates on our calendars. But what might Christmas become if we each stopped long enough to ask ourselves: *What makes Christmas meaningful? What will Christmas hold for us? How can Christmas satisfy the deepest yearnings of our hearts?*

Perhaps learning about how Christmas celebrations evolved over the centuries will help us answer these questions.

Back to the Basics:
Looking at Christmas History

Despite the fact that the Gospel of Luke links the date of Jesus' birth to a census in Palestine decreed by Caesar Augustus (Luke 2:1), nothing is known of the time of year of his birth. The first evidence of speculation about the date is in the third century when Clement of Alexandria suggested May 20. The earliest mention of observance on December 25 is in the Philocalian Calendar, representing Roman practice in the year 336. At about the same time, the Eastern church began to observe the Nativity on January 6, the feast of Epiphany. By the middle of the fifth century, however, most Eastern churches had adopted December 25.

As with other Christian holy days, the date of Christmas appears to have been set to provide an alternative to one or more popular pagan festivals. December 25 was originally the date of the feast to the sun god, Mithras. The cult of Mithras had spread from Persia into the Roman world in the first century, and by the third century was Christianity's main rival. December 25 also came at the end of the feast of Saturnalia, an ancient Roman festival commemorating the golden age of Saturn. Both of these festivals may well have been related to even earlier festivals marking the winter solstice.

Although Christmas was intended as an alternative to pagan festivals, the practices of those festivals were often simply incorporated into the Christian celebration. As Christianity spread through central and northern Europe, the accretions from local religions continued. As early as the fifth century, a small minority of Christian leaders expressed alarm at the growing pagan character of Christmas, a cause for concern that continued through the Middle Ages.

Christmas celebrations were not only enlarged by absorbing elements from local religions but from other Christian traditions as well, for example, St. Nicholas. The association of Christmas with St. Nicholas came about in the Middle Ages, especially in northern Europe. Little is known about his history except that he was Bishop of Myra in Asia Minor in the fourth century. Of the many stories about this saint, one of the most popular tells about his generosity in giving gifts anonymously to the poor. He became the patron saint of numerous countries, cities and groups, and especially of children. Because of this special relationship, tradition developed that he gave gifts to children on the eve of his feast day, December 6.

During the Reformation of the 16th century, many reformers wanted Christmas dropped as a Christian celebration. In their view, not only was there no biblical sanction for Christmas, but its popular practices still looked too much like the old Saturnalia festivals. In their general resistance to things Catholic, they also wanted St. Nicholas banished. For a few years in 17th-century England, the Puritan-dominated parliament outlawed the feast of Christmas. At the same time, Puritans in Massachusetts passed similar legislation. Between the 16th and 18th centuries, the widespread antipathy to Christmas as a holy day – especially by Puritans, Quakers, Baptists, and Presbyterians – had important consequences, consequences which those religious groups could not have imagined.

Resistance to attaching religious significance to Christmas encouraged its growth as a secular holiday. For example, St. Nicholas was replaced by a more secular figure known as Christmas Man, Father Christmas, and Papa Noël. The Dutch, reluctant to give up St. Nicholas, brought Sinterklass (St. Nicholas) with them when they came to America and honored him on December 6. In the 17th century, when the Dutch lost control of New Amsterdam to the English, Sinterklass was gradually anglicized into Santa Claus and acquired many of the accoutrements of Christmas Man – the workshop at the North Pole and the sleigh with reindeer. By the 19th century, when the formerly-resistant Protestant groups began to celebrate Christmas, it was not only a religious holy day but a well-established secular holiday as well.

The 20th Century: Commercialized Christmas

Through the 20th century in Europe and North America, the popular celebration of Christmas remains an amalgam of Christian and non-Christian traditions. The lack of clarity about the celebration's purpose has remained, accentuating a new factor in the 20th century: the commercialization of Christmas.

More than just a mixture of diverse traditions, Christmas is now big business. While the Christian calendar calls for a solemn four- or five-week preparation to celebrate the birth of Christ, the "Christmas economy" overshadows even Halloween, with Thanksgiving Day in the U.S. serving as little more than a prelude to the greatest shopping weekend of the year. In 1939, President Roosevelt moved the date of Thanksgiving back to the third Thursday of November to expand the Christmas shopping season. With the survival of many businesses dependent on Christmas profits and half of the annual advertising dollar spent on Christmas-related advertising, it is not surprising that for some shoppers Christmas spending is regarded as a patriotic duty.

The commercialization of Christmas did not occur in a social vacuum. It is part of our society in which consumption for its own sake – regardless of need – is legitimated and encouraged. Without reluctance, consumerism exploits religious beliefs and deep emotions to persuade people to buy. Advertising's behavior modification specialists demonstrate that the strains of *Joy to the World* trumpeting throughout the shopping malls in December produce greater profits, and that *Silent Night, Holy Night* is even better. Using Christmas as a religion-sanctioned occasion for extravagant spending, businesses hope that the practice of spending billions of dollars on Christmas gifts in North America is simply practice for greater spending throughout the rest of the year.

While it may be good for the economy in the short run, commercialized Christmas also has its costs. Preparations for observing the birth of one whose coming is "good news to the poor," are often displaced by the more financially attractive preparations to observe the coming of Santa Claus. Extravagant Christmas spending means fewer dollars available for those ministries and agencies addressing critical social and environmental problems. And the loss is more than dollars. The sense of exploitation that many feel at Christmas, the depression that comes when Christmas does not deliver the happiness popular hype promises, and the guilt from being willing participants in a religious fraud, all rob Christmas of its power to renew the human spirit.

Perhaps the greatest cost of commercialization at Christmas is paid by the poor. In our society, the poor experience Christmas as a cruel hoax. Our pervasive cultural Christmas ideology is not Christology – celebrating Christ's coming as "good news to the poor" – but what we might call "Santology."

The creed of Santa Claus theology is the well-known song, *Santa Claus is Coming to Town*. According to this creed, Santa is omniscient; like God, Santa knows all about us. There is also a day of judgment. It comes once a year when "good" children (and adults!) are rewarded with good things, while the "bad" (i.e., the poor) get coals and switches. The truth is, of course, that gifts are not distributed based on who has been "good or bad" or "naughty or nice," but on what people can afford or get credit to buy. But that's not what our culture teaches children.

What it teaches is bad for both poor and non-poor children. Poor children are told that they don't receive gifts because they are bad, while the non-poor are taught that they receive gifts because they are good. Both notions, equally reprehensible, are part of this culture's Santa Claus theology.

Commercial Christmas, its underpinnings of Santa Claus firmly in place, continues its spiraling growth. It seems evident that its cultural pervasiveness makes future change little less than a distant dream. It is also true that many Christians and congregations accept the distortion of their holy day without challenge. The reason, one suspects, is not so much an insensitivity to the issues, but rather a feeling of impotence – not knowing what to do or how to do it. Aware that slogans such as "putting Christ back in Christmas," and ideas about "Christmas basket charity" are simplistic, many opt to do nothing.

But does it have to be that way? Isn't there another choice?

Simplicity – at Christmas and Year-Round

As we approach a new millennium, thousands of North Americans are moving beyond materialistic values and choosing an outwardly more simple, inwardly more rich lifestyle. The phenomenon could foreshadow a major transformation in Western values, with wide implications for future developments in business, technology, and society at large. Some of these moves are made as companies downsize, forcing employees to rethink their futures. Others come about from an inner longing for something more.

In their essay "Voluntary Simplicity: Lifestyle of the Future?", Duane S. Elgin and Arnold Mitchell define the movement as embracing "frugality of consumption, a strong sense of environmental urgency, a desire to return to living and working environments which are of a more human scale, and an intention to realize our higher human potential – both psychological and spiritual – in community with others." Reusing and recycling, cutting back on unnecessary spending, and reducing material possessions when possible are all ways of practicing a more simple lifestyle.

Christmas – that time of year when the holiday's original meaning gets overshadowed by commercialism – is a wonderful time to begin simplifying our lifestyles. And in doing so, we may find our lives immeasurably enriched.

By living more consciously as we plan our holiday celebrations, we can refresh our hearts, minds, and spirits – at Christmas, and year-round.

Making Traditions Work for You

Tradition is the framework on which our Christmas celebrations are built. One definition of tradition is "a long-established custom or practice that has the effect of an unwritten law." Many aspects of Christmas are shaped or affected by tradition – family, friends, food, gifts, decorations, activities and faith, to name a few. Tradition influences what we consider to be special Christmas foods, whether we open our presents on Christmas Eve or Christmas morning, when we put up our Christmas tree, whether we have a manger scene, and many other celebration details.

How has your Christmas celebration gotten its particular shape? A number of forces bring the elements of Christmas together for each of us.

Family history is probably the main one. We learn what Christmas is about and how to celebrate it as we learn so much else, from our family. Our family

Christmas provides us with numerous customs and habits ("We've always done it that way..."). These can range from whether church or presents come first, to what brand of candy goes in the dish in the hall. Whether big or small, some of our traditions have acquired power and emotional resonance for us and we feel very attached to them. Our family history may also bring us elements from our religious heritage and from our ethnic heritage.

Our local community and our church also influence the traditions we adopt. From local craft fairs to annual performances of the *Messiah*, our celebrations embrace community and church traditions.

Advertising and the marketplace affect every aspect of Christmas and have a power and pervasiveness similar to the family's. Like the family, the touch of advertising ranges from big to small, from the promise that if we buy and give the right presents all will be well, to the idea that these particular little green and red candies are the only thing possible for that dish in the hall.

Lastly, our own consideration about what our celebrations represent affects which traditions we choose to highlight.

Questions for reflection

1. What personal or family traditions come to mind when you think of Christmas? Have you modified these in any way over time?
2. Can you think of other aspects of Christmas celebrating besides those mentioned above?
3. Do some of your Christmas traditions seem like unwritten laws?

The most important things

Some aspects of Christmastime celebrations are listed below. Using the lines on the left, rank these elements with either a 1, 2 or 3 for level of importance to you.

_____	_____	Family
_____	_____	Faith
_____	_____	Friends
_____	_____	Activities
_____	_____	Food
_____	_____	Decorations
_____	_____	Gifts
_____	_____	Other

Reflect on your holiday as you ask the following questions, and on the lines below write down some of your own traditions:

FAMILY. Is your family involved in your Christmas planning? celebrating? Immediate family, extended family? Are there different Christmas roles for women and men? Are there different generations involved in your Christmas? Do you have to coordinate your family traditions with those of another family? Any conflicts with spouse, in-laws or ex-relatives? How much time do you spend together – hours, days, weeks? Do you travel or does family come to you? Are you happy with the balance between family and self at Christmas?

_____

_____

_____

_____

_____

_____

_____

_____

FRIENDS. Are your friends involved in your Christmas? In what ways? Do you share gifts, activities, meals, decorating? Do you send cards? Does sending cards foster your friendships with others? Do you reach out to distant friends at this time?

_____

_____

_____

_____

_____

_____

FOOD. What role does food play in your Christmas? Do you have special Christmas foods? Cookies, meals, party foods? How much time and money does food preparation take? Do you share food? With whom?

_____

_____

_____

_____

_____

_____

GIFTS. How are gifts – planning, requesting, purchasing or making, wrapping, delivering, opening, paying – woven through your Christmas sea-

son? What role does Santa play in your Christmas? Does charity have a part in your gift-giving?

_____

_____

_____

_____

_____

DECORATIONS. Do you decorate your home and life at Christmas? If you have a tree, is it live, cut or artificial? What about a wreath or other greens? Advent wreath, manger scene? Candles? Ornaments? Cards?

_____

_____

_____

_____

_____

_____

ACTIVITIES. What activities are part of your Christmas season? Is Christmas a solitary time or do you spend it with family or friends? When does the season start and end for you? What kinds of programs and events – school, church, community, religious, games or sports,

TV specials, social activities or parties – do you participate in?

_____

_____

_____

_____

_____

_____

FAITH. How is God present in all of your Christmas celebrating? What part does Jesus have in your Christmas? How is God present for you personally? As a family, community, or church member? How is God present in your home? In your activities, use of money and time, food, gifts?

_____

_____

_____

_____

_____

_____

_____

OTHERS. Perhaps these questions have reminded you of other elements that define Christmas for you.

_____

_____

_____

_____

_____

_____

_____

_____

_____

Go back through the elements again and ask yourself why each item is included. Is it meaningful to you? Do you do it out of choice or obligation, or both? Does it represent habit, family tradition, religious expression, commercial pressure?

Now go back to your rankings on page 19. Using the lines on the right, rank the elements 1, 2 or 3 according to how much time and energy you devote to them.

More reflection

1. Consider the two rankings you listed at the beginning – what was important to you and what took your time and energy. Are the things that are most important to you also the things you devote most of your time and energy to?

2. Think about the whole that these elements make. How does it feel to you emotionally? Is it spiritu-

ally fulfilling? What do you think about your holiday in light of what you know about yourself and God?

3. Which parts of your celebration are pleasing and balanced to you?

4. Which ones are meaningless or troublesome?

5. Which would be fine with a little reworking?

6. Do any themes or patterns emerge in the group's celebration traditions?

What To Do when Christmas Is Chaos

A picture-perfect Christmas is rarely experienced in our society. Christmas is anything but calm. Often, it is a time of exhaustion. There are simply too many parties and activities to attend, too many gifts to buy, too many cookies to bake, too many decorations to hang and too many rooms to clean. When Christmas Day arrives, we often feel relief rather than abundant joy.

Christmas is also a time of depression and guilt. Bombarded with media images of a "good" Christmas and faced with strained budgets and uneasy family situations, our celebrations rarely fulfill the media's ideal. And when Christmas is over, we can feel immense guilt that we've let ourselves and our celebration of this holy day be exploited once again.

When faced with pressures from our culture, the marketplace, our families and even ourselves, we can forget whose birthday we celebrate. Unrealistic expectations and demands can rob Christmas of its power to renew the human spirit.

But what can we do? Although there are no miraculous remedies, we *can* find ways to resist cultural pressures and to focus our celebrations on the birth of Christ.

What you can do

- **Decide that something must be done.** Just think of all the times when only a few people made a critical difference in the life of a church, a community, or even a nation. Deciding that change is important is the first and most fundamental step in using this resource.

- **Find others who share your concerns.** Share this book with a few friends and discuss your concerns. You will probably run into a few people who are uninterested, or even opposed, but you will also find those who are just waiting for someone to lead them. Get those who are interested together as soon as possible, and start an alternative Christmas committee.

- **Be persistent.** Foot-dragging occurs whenever a committee is formed. When presented with a new idea, committees have been known to talk it to death. Be patient and understanding in dealing with people's doubts and fears. Don't be self-righteous, but be persistent!

At home

- **Restrict exposure to media.** Use the weeks before Christmas to develop a "spirituality of cultural resistance." Watch less television. Spend less time in shopping malls. Throw away (recycle) Christmas catalogs.

- **Simplify your celebrations.** Cut out unnecessary activities. Don't overburden yourself with Christmas events and preparations. Let your Advent activities focus on preparing for the birth of Christ, not on preparing for a lavish celebration. Set limits and stick to them.

- **Turn to activities which are less consumer-oriented.** Spend time in personal, quiet reflection. Spend time with family, friends and those in need. Use the ideas in Part One of this book with those in your household or small group. Set aside time each day to use the Advent Calendars and Reflections in Part Two.

- **Remember those whom Christ came to serve.** Give gifts appropriate to the celebration of Christ's birth. Remember the hungry, the thirsty, the naked and the imprisoned in your holiday gift-giving. Make meaningful gifts for family and friends. Give of your time and talents. Invite persons to set aside an amount equal to 25% of what they spent on last year's Christmas and give it as a "birthday present" to those in need. (See the section on Simple Gift-Giving, page 27).

You may want to suggest that this money be set aside daily or weekly in a container on the table where the family eats. Encourage participants to make their "birthday presents." Include things other than money too, such as year-long commitments of time and skill to ministries aiding those in need.

(Note: This is not a fund-raising scheme, nor is it a glorified "Christmas Basket" approach to dealing with poverty. It is a way for individuals and families to honor the one whose birth they are celebrating by diverting money and time that they would otherwise spend on themselves and friends.)

• **Involve the children.** Although they may be the family members most susceptible to society's commercialized Christmas propaganda, children can be an important part of the household's resistance. Children understand what birthdays are supposed to be, so they will be able to grasp the concept of Christmas as Jesus' birthday. In addition, the open-mindedness of most children can often influence adults who may be a bit jaded and cynical.

Many of the resources in this book can involve children. Encourage children to participate in the Advent services. Set aside time for the household activities.

In your church or community

• **Make Alternatives' booklet *Whose Birthday Is It, Anyway?* available to all households in your parish.** If you don't have the money in your church's budget to purchase booklets, you can ask each family to "pitch in" or you can plan a fundraising event or special offering.

Unless the patterns of Christmas preparation are changed in the household, significant change elsewhere is unlikely. The struggle over the commercialization of Christmas is won or lost in the home. Popular culture's values pour into our living rooms and children's minds, especially through the television. Unless there are efforts *in the household* to counter this flood of propaganda, mass culture is sure to win. This book offers positive and creative activities to counter social pressures.

• **Encourage Christmas stewardship.** Call attention to alternative giving for your group as well as yourself.

• **Plan other Christmas events in your church.** Offer support for families and individuals who are trying to resist cultural pressures by planning special Christmas plays, presentations, study groups or gatherings in the church.

• **Organize an adult study of the Advent texts** during the four weeks of Advent. The biblical reflections in Part Two of this book probe these familiar texts to uncover what they say about our Christmas preparations. Make sure that each member of your group has a copy of the study. (Note: Any piece in this book is available in quantity from Alternatives.)

• **Don't stop with Christmas.** If Christmas is near, Easter can't be far behind. Bunnies and baskets will soon fill the shelves so recently vacated by Santa Claus. The significance of the death and resurrection of Christ is often overshadowed by colored eggs and new finery. Begin now to think about the changes you can make during Lent and Easter.

Simple Gift-Giving

What can I give Him,
Poor as I am?
If I were a shepherd
I would bring a lamb,
If I were a Wise Man
I would do my part,
Yet what can I give Him?
Give my heart.
Christina Rossetti

Guidelines for Alternative Giving

We know many Christmas stories about the perfect gift: the tender sacrifice for the combs and watch fob in O. Henry's story the "Gift of the Magi"; the shoemaker offering hospitality to an old man, an old woman, a poor mother and child as he waits for Christ to visit; the peasant going to honor baby Jesus, offering his intended gift to a poor child along the way; the huge satisfaction and celebration of the Cratchits with their meager Christmas dinner. And in the second chapter of Matthew, there are the magi who followed the star to bring their gifts to baby Jesus. From these and other stories we understand the essence of gifts and giving. Gifts come from the heart. God is in our neighbor. Joy is not in how much we have, but in how we share and celebrate.

As Christmas approaches, does this knowledge become overshadowed? Do malls, catalogs, advertisements and external pressure provide the ideas and substance of *our* gifts and giving? Do Santa's gifts overpower God's gifts?

"God can see everything, so God tells Santa who's been bad and good," said one four-year-old. What do our attitudes and gifts have in common with those stories that so touch our hearts? What do we have to give? The magi had three gifts. Like them, we also have three gifts we can bring at Christmas: our *time*, our *talent* and our *money*.

North American commercialism dictates a basic structure for gifts and giving: we use our time and sometimes our talent earning money. We then spend money and our time to purchase objects made by others. We give these gifts to our family and friends. We might make a donation to charity, a money gift for the poor. We honor Jesus at our various church services, and – that's Christmas!

But what do those Christmas stories tell us about giving? Gifts come from the heart. God is in our neighbor. There is joy in sharing and celebrating. We can arrange the kinds of gifts (time, talent and money) and those we gift (Jesus, family and friends, the poor, and our neighbor) in a kaleidoscope of ways. We can ask, who needs what from me? How can I give in ways that honor the birth of Jesus?

Time

For many of us, the gift of time is a precious and costly gift indeed. With our busy lives, to give our time as a present, or use our time to make a present, can be sacrificial giving. For Christmas, a salesman father gave his son one hour an evening, every day he was home. The son could choose the activity. This gift became so important to both of them that they renewed it the next Christmas.

A husband gave his musical wife a day alone with her cello while he took the children on an outing – this gift touched more than one person!

A mother divided the pages of a "Day at a Glance" calendar for the upcoming year and sent them to her daughter's friends and relatives, who wrote thoughts, memories, jokes and anecdotes and mailed them back. This mother reassembled the calendar and presented it to her daughter, who found herself looking forward to each day's message.

A son and family visited his older parents before Christmas. As their gift they brought a platter of homemade cookies and candy and spent the day repairing the roof and mulching the garden for winter.

We can offer time to celebrate family connections and history. Create a photo collage for a distant grandparent. Tape and duplicate family events, special moments, an elder's memories. Tape yourself reading a story for young relatives, or recount stories from your own childhood.

We can commit to a schedule of regular phone calls, letters, visits – whatever our mode and circumstances – as a gift for someone we care about.

We can volunteer regularly for a given amount of time, either as a gift to those directly served or as a gift in honor of someone else. One woman prepares Christmas breakfast in her home for everyone she knows who is alone that Christmas.

Talent

Artistic talents can yield pictures, cards and stationery, music and song, small books or stories. One young woman created a sampler for her grandmother picturing all the grandchildren.

We can look in everyday places to draw on the talents we take for granted: sewing, cooking, gardening, carpentry, repair work. One friend hates to mend; another finds an evening of mending soothing. One woman prepared a gift basket with checkered napkins, homemade spaghetti and sauce, and breadsticks. A woman gave a year of good wishes to her parents – 365 messages in a box from which they could choose one each day.

A gift of time combines with talent when we make gifts, by ourselves or with our children. A child can draw pictures or sort photographs for a photocopied calendar. Tiles, grout, and a piece of masonite make trivets that last for years. Folded origami cranes make gifts of peace to decorate the trees of friends and neighbors.

Money

The point of alternative giving is not primarily to stop giving or to stop spending money but, once again, to remember that essential knowledge: gifts come from the heart. We find God in our neighbor. Joy comes not from how much we have, but from how we share and celebrate.

We can combine our money with thoughtfulness to truly give gifts from the heart. Three children pooled money to replace their mom's recently lost wedding ring, a cherished memento of their deceased father. A son gave his parents two framed pictures, drawn by an artist from photos, of the farm houses in which they each grew up. A husband gave his wife a video, copied from home movies, of her parents' 1932 wedding. One year, a religious community went without Christmas gifts at all and gave the money to a sister community whose need was great.

We can honor Jesus and share with our neighbors both locally and around the world by giving money to organizations that serve various needs. In Matthew 25, Jesus tells us that, in order to give to him, we must find him in the hungry, the thirsty, the sick, the naked, the imprisoned. We can share a portion of our usual Christmas spending – say 25% – as a special gift to those in need. These donations can also be given in a loved one's name as our gift to them. The Christmas after one woman underwent cataract surgery, her family donated money in her name to a program which sponsors eye surgery in Ghana. We can buy hams for a soup kitchen's Christmas meal, or blankets for a shelter, or art supplies for a homeless children's art program. One family spent their Christmas holiday together building a house for Habitat for Humanity.

Like the magi, we have three Christmas gifts: our time, talent and money. The magi traveled far and searched hard to bring their gifts to the one whose birth we celebrate. Their story has become part of our celebration. This year, write your own story of Christmas giving.

Use this space to jot down your ideas.

Time _____

_____

_____

_____

Talent _____

_____

_____

Money _____

_____

_____

_____

Reclaiming Christmas

"My peace I give to you.
I do not give to you as the world gives.
Do not let your hearts be troubled."
John 14:27

This Christmas, we would all like to have the peace of Christ, the ability to give as Jesus gave, and hearts that are not troubled. These hopes are at the heart of alternative giving!

My peace I give to you

In our consumer society, it's easy to forget that Christmas is the celebration of Jesus' birth. With so much emphasis on giving and receiving presents, Christ's gift of peace to us can get lost or forgotten. This year,

1. **Experience the peace of Christ**
   Schedule a period of time each day during Advent to be alone and to pray and study the scriptures. Allow God to prepare you for the coming of the Prince of Peace.

2. **Share the peace of Christ**
   We can give a birthday gift to Jesus. Read Matthew 25:31-40. Jesus insists giving to him means giving to the hungry, the thirsty, the stranger, the sick and the imprisoned. Consider pledging 25% of what you normally spend on Christmas gifts to organizations that serve those in need. Pledge to volunteer your time in a community program through the coming year.

I do not give as the world gives

After the Christmas season, many people find themselves deep in debt, having spent hundreds of dollars for presents they cannot really afford. Cultural pressures, trying to meet expectations, or perhaps simply a desire to be loved can be powerful motivations to spend beyond our means. Before you begin your Christmas shopping, consider the following:

1. **Take control of your spending** Read 2 Corinthians 9:5-7. God loves a "cheerful giver," but the text also says "give as you have made up your mind ... not under compulsion." Don't buy anything you can't pay for this December.

2. **Use the *Plan Your Gift-Giving!* guide** (following this section). Don't look at catalogs or go window shopping for gift ideas. Instead, begin by thinking about the person to whom you want to give. What message would you like your gift to communicate? The best gifts are ones that share our time and talents; ones that truly express the love and commitment we have made to family, friends and our community.

3. **Consider the messages gifts bring.** The gifts we share say something about the values we hold dear. Advertisers, for example, would have us believe that violent games and toy guns make ideal Christmas gifts. But what do games associated with war and killing have to do with celebrating the coming of the Prince of Peace?

Do not let your hearts be troubled

Give to yourself. Before the Christmas rush begins and the course of events begins to control you, consider ways you can bring comfort to your troubled heart.

1. **Reflect.** Think about your past Christmas celebrations. What is it about Christmas and gift-giving that you found frustrating or troubling? Make a list. Give your conscience time to be heard!

2. **Share.** Discuss your feelings with household members or friends. See if you can find other people in your church or community who want to change their giving habits.

Remember, your Christmas giving can both honor Christ's birth and show your love and concern for others.

Plan Your Gift-Giving!

Below are sample questions (and responses for a sample person) that you can use as you plan your Christmas gift for a particular person.

1. Who is this person to me?

   • *My sister-in-law.*

2. How well do I know her?

   • *Pretty well, not in an everyday way. We can talk deeply when we see each other.*

3. How much a part of each other's lives are we?

   • *We see each other once or twice a year.*

4. What's important to her?

   • *Writing, reading, bicycles, her family and community, neighborhood activism, personal self-awareness.*

5. What does she like?

   • *New York City (where she lives), socializing, clothes, movies, cooking, sewing and other handicrafts, writing, doing special things for her husband and baby.*

6. What's going on in her life now and in the last year?

   • *Her first baby. An ongoing writing class. Balancing free-lance writing and child care needs.*

7. How do I see God working in her life right now?

   • *Reconciliation with birth family through the baby.*

8. What various roles does she play in her life?

- *Part-time worker, free-lance writer, wife, mom, neighborhood activist.*

9. Could she use special support in any of these roles?

- *Free-lance writer, mom roles. Dealing with the isolation of motherhood.*

10. What are her "growing edges"?

- *Learning a new perspective on her self-involvement. Learning about the "mom" role.*

11. What could help a particular activity in her life?

- *Child care. Short things to read.*

12. What interests or activities do we share?

- *Balancing work and motherhood. Reading and writing. Handwork.*

13. What do I admire about her?

- *Her sense of humor and playfulness, acts of caring for her husband, her fitness, her personal organization.*

14. What values do I want to express?

- *Support, connection, simplicity, world consciousness.*

15. What would give me pleasure to find for her?

- *A book, a special event of some kind, something about exploring NYC, jewelry, picture frame or photo album, something creative.*

16. What could say to her, "Through your living I see that certain values are important to you. I want

- *Gifts connected to her interests. I could support her sense of community and fondness for socializing and*

to support and celebrate that in you."? *also address her isolation by calling her once a month.*

17. Are there gifts from alternative sources that I could consider for this person?

   • *Jewelry and scarves from third world producers, food products.*

18. Let intuition and imagination do some work: brainstorm ideas. How could I make her a gift of my time? talent or skill? money? What can I get that's appropriate for the amount I can spend?

   • *Dave Barry book, subscription to literary magazine (short pieces easily read by a busy mom), money for her writing class, offer to layout a neighborhood flyer for her on my computer and fax it to her, donation to the literacy group she used to volunteer for, commitment to a year of phone calls once a month.*

After you have some ideas, consider these thoughts
- How could any of these gifts foster God's work in her life?
- Are any of these ideas a gift to God as well?
- What do each of these gift ideas communicate about my understanding of myself and the world?
- Where can I find such an item? Who would know where I could find it?
- Could I make it?
- Does a meaningful gift have to cost a lot?
- If it's too expensive for me alone, can I organize others to go in on it with me?
- Can I purchase it from a locally-owned store rather than from a chain? Can I get a used one?
- How do prices compare between driving to get it, wrapping and shipping it myself and having it shipped from a catalog company?

The Best – and Worst – Gifts

A gift of talent

The best Christmas present I ever received was a modern sampler picture made by my oldest granddaughter, who is 19. Embroidered in old English lettering is the word "Grandma" in black on a white background. Over each letter are little figures, done in tiny cross stitching, of my 12 grandchildren each in a pose depicting his or her interest. They are ready to dive, to dance and to play soccer. One is acting in a play, another gardening and one is simply relaxing. Even the children's hair is their true coloring. Above each head is the child's name.

My children's families live far away from me. Having this lovely picture on my kitchen wall is a wonderful and constant reminder of each of them.

A gift of time

I am a salesman and spend a fair amount of time on the road. I decided that I would give my son a Christmas gift that would last a year, or possibly a lifetime. I gave him an hour of my time every evening that I was home. He could do anything he wanted to with me for that hour. We did all sorts of unique things – played games, took rides, read to each other, built models – but most importantly, we talked. We talked about everything from what I wanted to be when I was his age to why I chose the occupation I did, to why I married his mother.

I learned about my son's fears and concerns. And we both learned how important it is to have quality time with each other. As we approach the new Christmas season, we have decided to renew our gift. I would hope that other parents might choose this gift as one to give to their children, or for that matter, to each other.

A gift of memories

On Thanksgiving Day as our guests were leaving, my sister handed me a small wrapped package, saying, "Put this aside until later." She gave a similar package to another sister. I took the small wrapped box and tucked it away since my husband and I were going out-of-town the next morning.

On returning from our trip, I thought of that small package and decided to open it. Inside was a poem and a cassette recording. I put the cassette in the player, and to my surprise came the voices of our family singing Christmas carols, and most special of all, the voice of our mother, singing Silent Night (*Stille Nacht*) in German. Mother died this past September. She played piano and organ beautifully, and we children grew up with music filling our home.

What a wonderful gift to hear Mother's voice once again, and at this special Christmas season.

A thoughtful purchase

Last year I received the best Christmas present anyone could have given. My father died when I was young and for each of the last seven years I had spent Christmas in a different foster home. Each time I was with virtual strangers, and I never felt happy or loved. Last year was to be my first Christmas alone. My friend was spending the day with family in a nearby town when he called and told me he was coming to see me. When he arrived he told me to close

my eyes because he had a surprise for me. When I opened them, I was very touched because he had brought a little tree full of ornaments and lights. Words cannot express the feelings that were going through me. I was not able to afford a tree, yet I had a beautiful tree given to me. And I thought I would be spending Christmas alone.

All I had heard about Christmas came true. My friend did something very sweet and made someone who had felt unloved and alone feel just the opposite. Love – that was the best present I ever received.

The calendar

The Christmas gift I received from my mom last year was great! It required a lot of careful planning and effort. Early in the fall she purchased a desk calendar (the kind with two rings and loose-leaf 3 x 4 sheets which are flipped over daily). Mom removed the individual sheets and sent two to five pages to people (of all ages) who are important to me. Each person was instructed to contribute a little message of any kind to me, and return the pages to her office. By mid-December, she had received the pages back, and was able to reassemble my special calendar.

Imagine what joy it has brought me to hear from my wonderful friends and family members each day of the year. Every day brings a new surprise. Many people wrote about memories, others wrote words of inspiration, jokes or guesses as to what I would be doing on that particular date. Starting each day with a message from a special someone has been wonderful.

Somebody else's middle name

The worst Christmas gift that I received was from my mother-in-law. She gave me a monogrammed sweater. She did not know my middle name, so she picked a letter out herself to fill the space. (I've only been married for 15 years.) I never wore the sweater because I felt it belonged to someone else.

Wrapping paper with meaning

A framed piece of Christmas wrapping paper was the best gift I ever received. About 25 years ago, my husband was given a very large roll of wrapping paper from his family's bakery that was going out of business. The paper had been used to wrap the bread, cookies and cakes they made. It became a family tradition to wrap at least one gift each Christmas with this paper.

Last year, in memory of past happy Christmases and in memory of my recently deceased husband, my grandson sent each family member a framed piece of this wrapping paper saved from previous years. The originality, thoughtfulness and ingenuity of this gift expressed my grandson's love for his late grandfather and for his family.

A pang of conscience

My worst Christmas gift was a last minute "pang of conscience" gift from my husband. Goaded by an in-law who had purchased his spouse a magnificent diamond, my hubby evidently dashed through the local Five & Dime store, grabbing anything he saw. There was an atrocious kerosene lamp with a putrid red base, a pair of knee stockings which varicose veins had never permitted me to wear, a short plastic man's style comb, a can of hairspray to which I was allergic, a pair of underwear three sizes too large, a cheap cardboard picture of a man sitting in a boat fishing while puffing on a cigar, and a pen inscribed, "Buy at the Best for Less."

However, to my love's credit, all of the items were somewhat gift-wrapped in a haphazard manner in a patchwork of assorted designs bearing messages such as "Happy Birthday," "Congratulations," "Good Luck," etc. by wadding the tissue around the gift and plastering it with scotch tape. All were dumped in a box from the grocery store. He could not understand why I was not ecstatic.

The gold ring

The best gift I received last Christmas was a wedding ring from my three children. During the fall, while working in the yard and woods, somehow the wedding ring I had worn for 46 years slipped off my finger. The ground around my home is covered with layers of pine straw and mulch. All my searching was unsuccessful.

Since my husband had died the year before, I was heartbroken. All fall I silently mourned the bare finger with the obvious wedding ring indentation. It felt and looked so strange!

Imagine my joy Christmas morning when I found a replacement ring with a note, from three wonderfully sensitive and caring children, which said: "We know this isn't the best – but maybe it's next best. With our love."

Diamonds aren't forever

The worst gift I have ever received was a pair of 1/4 carat diamond earrings, expensively wrapped and tucked into my Christmas stocking by my husband.

That year my Christmas wish list asked for his time, time to talk together and truly share our lives; his patience when our world is rumbling with the stresses of everyday life; his love to conquer all life's little wrinkles.

Instead my Christmas gift had the cold twinkle of commercial Christmas. We are divorced now.

The umbrella

This is the worst gift I ever received. As a post-polio victim I have walked on a pair of crutches for many, many years. Would you believe my boss gave me an umbrella for Christmas?

An invitation

The best Christmas present I received last year was from my niece and her husband. It was an invitation to spend time at their home until I was well enough to care for myself. I had just had open heart surgery. No money can buy the joy I received from that precious gift.

What Is a Gift?

A Reflection/Action Resource

Carolyn Hardin Engelhardt

Carolyn Hardin Engelhardt serves as Director of Vieth Resource Center, The Divinity School, Yale University, New Haven, CT, and also as church program ministries consultant. She has written numerous resources for Alternatives.

What is a gift? Everyone knows the answer. Or do we? If it were an easy question with an easy answer, we wouldn't need a resource such as this. Try asking a few people of various ages what a gift is. You will probably be surprised at the answers you get.

It seems almost antithetical to say that giving a gift is hard or challenging or demanding, but that may be our experience. It's hard to know for sure when a gift to someone is *not* a gift, but a bribe, a self-congratulation, or actually a gift to oneself. It is difficult to make the process of choosing gifts and giving gifts consistent with our faith. Because living our faith is challenging and demanding, giving gifts

that come from our faith – from whatever depth, breadth and authenticity our faith has – is also challenging. So, what is a gift? What is giving?

Giving gifts to loved ones has not always been a central part of Christmas. Could it be that we associate them with one another now because something in our spirit wants to integrate what is meaningful into a cohesive whole?

At one time or another, almost everyone has been troubled by something concerning gifts and presents. That disequilibrium makes very fertile soil for growing in personal faith and for transforming lives. There may be moments of risk, embarrassment and lack of clarity as we examine our lives and gifts. Remember, gifts from God are ready for us to receive as we consider "What is a gift?" Use some of these reflection experiences to explore gifts and giving.

Reflection experience one: "A gift is ... "

Mark each of the following statements TRUE or FALSE. If you are doing this exercise as an individual, write your answers down on a piece of paper. If you mark a statement FALSE, change it so that you could say it is TRUE. Do so by choosing one of the following words to substitute for "gift" in the statements below: present, bribe, tribute, sacrifice, donation, favor, bounty, contribution, gratuity, tip, charity, or remuneration.

"Every good thing bestowed and every perfect gift is from above ... " (James 1:17)

A gift is

____ something the receiver wants
____ something that fits the person's personality
____ something the receiver would not get for herself or himself
____ something the person would enjoy
____ something that shows I was thinking about the person
____ something that reminds me of that person
____ something that is a part of me
____ something that will make a positive contribution to the world as the person uses it
____ sharing something of myself
____ letting a person know something that I admire about them through my gift
____ a contribution to that person's well-being, personal development or growth
____ a contribution to someone's well-being through the payment for the gift
____ an affirmation of someone's culture
____ an affirmation of an individual's lifestyle
____ something that promotes peace, justice and well-being for all creation
____ a responsible use of the world's resources
____ something that can be understood as coming from God's grace
____ something I am required to give

___ something I am not obligated to give

___ something that builds relation-ships

___ something that can be viewed as "doing a favor"

___ not earned

___ not deserved

___ an offering

___ a reward

___ not a reward

___ contains concepts that I believe are important

___ something whose full meaning cannot necessarily be seen

___ something whose cost has an implied message

___ something that shows my hos-pitality

___ something that conveys an un-derstanding of our relationship

___ something that is given without expecting something in return

___ something that cements a rela-tionship

___ something given anonymously

___ equal to other gifts given

___ is most appropriate when there is one in exchange for mine

___ unusual between persons who do not know each other

___ given in return for favors re-ceived

___ given in anticipation of favors

___ something appropriate to the status of the recipient

___ proportionate to the blessings we have received from God

___ an opportunity for reflection

___ not a gift if there is any injus-tice involved in its production or acquisition

___ something that implies reci-procity

___ something that helps us deal with our guilt and sin

___ a gift only if the giver is aware of any cost to humanity that it involves

___ renewing

___ sometimes a sacrifice

___ always an offering

___ part of our stewardship of re-sources

___ a thanksgiving

___ based on merit

___ related to a tithe

___ a prayer we can see

___ one's response to God

___ not something we ask for

___ an evidence of God's spirit

___ free

___ something that indicates that we know we belong to God

___ an opportunity for us to acknowledge that all we have is really God's

___ something that shows that everyone deserves to have material well-being

___ an acknowledgment that there is enough for all

Reflection experience two:
What is giving a gift?

1. Think about a gift you have given.

2. What were the consequences for you and for the receiver of your giving that gift.

3. Read the story of the announcement of God's gift in Luke 1:26-38.

4. Compare your experience of giving a gift to God's experience of giving a gift to Mary. What is similar and what is different?

5. What response does this comparison call for?

Reflection experience three:
Is it really a gift?

1. Have you ever given or received something that was called a gift but really seemed more like a tribute, homage, reward, bounty, bribe or trade? Describe (or draw) the experience.

2. Describe (or draw) the results, outcomes, or consequences of that experience for you or for others.

3. Read the following passages (you may want to read from several translations and read what comes before and after to understand the context) – Psalm 72:10; 2 Samuel 8:2 and 6; Psalm 45:12; Matthew 17:24-27; Proverbs 15:27; Ecclesiastes 7:7; Exodus 23:8.

4. In comparing the experience that you drew or described with those read about in the Bible, what similarities to or differences from your experience do you see?

"... it was of their own accord that they made their gift, which was not merely as far as their resources would allow, but well beyond their resources; ... it began by their offering themselves to the Lord and to us at the prompting of the will of God" (2 Corinthians 8:3, 5).

5. As you consider your experience in dialogue with that in the scriptures, what does God's spirit call forth from you in response?

Reflection experience four:
What is a gift?

1. Write each of these words on a separate card: gift, present, offering, sacrifice. Now, using four more cards, write your definition of each of the above words.

2. Now take the "gift" word card and write down how you might feel or what you might do if you thought of something as a gift. Do the same with the "present" card, with the "sacrifice" card, and with the "offering" card.

3. Read the following scriptures: Numbers 18:8-19; Ecclesiastes 3:12-13; Ecclesiastes 5:17-19; James 1:16-17; 2 Corinthians 9:6-15; Matthew 5:23-25; Matthew 23:13-32; 2 Corinthians 8:1-6; Deuteronomy 16:16-17; Amos 5:21-27.

4. Compare your definitions with what you read in the scripture references. How are your definitions similar to or different from the understandings of these words in biblical times?

5. As you think about your understanding of the words you defined as well as what you read in the scrip-

tures, in what way do you feel called to respond? Are you called to give *gifts* only? Is it okay to give bribes, offerings or sacrifices at times? Are all of these words appropriate descriptions of what Christians might do at some time? Why?

Reflection experience five:
Suggestions for giving a gift

Before reading this list, or sharing it with others, read Acts 3:1-10. Think about this passage and how it compares to the giving we may do at Christmas. How is it like our culture's giving at Christmas? How is it different from our culture's giving at Christmas? What response does it call for from us?

1. Before buying a gift, think about the person to whom you plan to give the gift. What does the person value? What does s/he care about? Really give time to think about that person. What can you do to affirm that person's individuality, creativity, concerns, lifestyle? What can you do to extend that person's concerns? What can you do to make it easier or more meaningful for them to live the life that embodies their values?

"But Peter said, 'I do not possess silver and gold, but what I do have I give to you: in the name of Jesus Christ the Nazarene – walk!'" (Acts 3:6).

2. Only *after* reflecting on the individual should we ever look at catalogs and advertisements. You might say that catalogs are important for helping us know what is "out there" that this person might appreciate. That may be true, but reflecting on the individual should come first. (Consider seeking out those catalogs that supply products that make for peace, justice and well-being for all people and for all of the planet.)

3. Consider making a card to go along with the gift that shares your thoughts as you prepared to give the gift. You might say something like: "I thought about you and what you value and how you contribute to all of us. As I thought about you, I wanted to support what your life shows is important. This gift comes with my prayers and thanksgiving for who you are and my hope that this gift will enhance your way of living with us. Sincerely, Carolyn."

It may be that this note will be appreciated as much as or more than the gift itself.

4. Think about your understanding of gifts and giving. Repeat this every year as you change and grow as a person, renewing and reforming your commitments. If possible, discuss your ideas and commitments with others. In addition to finding support, you may also influence others' concerns. In any case, others will be more prepared to understand your choices even if they do not participate in those choices.

5. Think about or discuss your feelings about "grab bags," drawing names and gift exchanges at workplaces, clubs, church groups and organizations. Are these words consistent with the values you are trying to live by? If such practices are not consistent with your understanding of gifts and giving, do you raise those concerns with those in the group? Do you choose not to participate? Do you participate because you are part of the group? Finding ourselves in situations that are inconsistent with

our values calls for exploration and decision-making. Not talking about these concerns may mean that others miss an opportunity for feeling that they are doing what is most consistent with *their* values.

6. Remember that giving purchased gifts is not the only way to give a gift. If relatives or friends (even those with whom you are very close) live far away, buying items that may or may not fit into their home decor or personal wardrobe, or buying items that they do not need or are inconsistent with their interests at the time does not make sense. Consider discontinuing buying gifts for each other. With the resources you save, you might feel more free to spend time together, using visits as gifts to one another. You might also feel more free to give spontaneously when you think of an appropriate gift. I have found this a mutual and very appreciated decision in my birth family. We use our money to share meals and spend family recreation time together.

Reflection experience six: The time and place for Christmas giving

1. Do you, or should you, make gifts a primary focus?

2. Do you, or should you, make *giving* gifts a primary focus?

3. Do you make receiving gifts a primary focus?

4. Do you, or should you, start putting gifts out for all to see very early in the Christmas season? Do you put them under the tree days or weeks before Christmas? If so, what does that do to the focus of the Christmas season? Is that good?

5. Do we encourage people to make lists of "what I want for Christmas"? What is the effect of the practice?

6. Do we speak of "having Christmas" as the time when gifts are opened? Is that what we intend Christmas to mean?

"And they came into the house and saw the child with Mary his mother; and they fell down and worshipped him; and opening their treasures they presented to him gifts of gold, frankincense and myrrh" (Matthew 2:11).

7. What does the time when we open gifts say about our priorities concerning Christmas? What does it say about our priorities if we decide to open gifts on Christmas Eve, on Christmas morning, during Kwanzaa, on December 6th, on January 6th, or at some other time?

8. Does opening gifts prevent our participation in the worship and celebrations of our churches on Christmas Eve, on Christmas Day, or on Epiphany? (Does the gift of God to us all collectively mean that we should celebrate that gift in the presence of the congregation rather than only in some devotional experience in our homes?)

9. What reminders do we, or should we, have in our homes about God's gifts or about gifts for those other than close friends and family?

10. What should be the relationship between the Christmas tree and the nativity scene figures we might have in our homes?

Reflection experience seven: Questions to answer as we prepare to give a gift

1. What does this gift say about how I understand the one who will receive it?

2. What does this giving say about how I understand myself?

3. What does this gift say about how I understand the world?

4. What does this gift say about the poor and about our "share" in the world's resources?

5. Is this a gift to God as well as to the person receiving it?

6. What could I give that is not purchased?

7. Does this gift point toward justice and equality for all God's people?

8. What does this gift say I value?

9. Does this gift show that we are "not conforming to this world, but being transformed by God's spirit"?

10. Should job-related giving follow the same standards as giving that I do all alone?

"Do not model your behavior on the contemporary world, but let the renewing of your minds transform you, so that you may discern for yourselves what is the will of God

– what is good and acceptable and mature" (Romans 12:2).

11. Should my giving within community groups and organizations follow the standards I have for my personal giving? (Be aware of the corrupting possibilities of gifts: Proverbs 15:27, Ecclesiastes 7:7.)

War Toys and Christmas: a Contradiction in Terms

Rachel G. Gill

Rachel Gill, Alternatives' former editor, is now retired in Stone Mountain, GA, where she lives with husband Buddy.

This material on Christmas, children and violent toys is a reflection/action piece to help families, church groups and educators deal with a society that pushes militarism on its children through violence-oriented toys. It may be used as a resource for developing awareness and initiating action on the issues around war toys. We believe it will be especially helpful for parents of young children.

"No society interested in attaining peace and justice can allow militarization of the young to go unchallenged. Any vision of a future without war and mass killing is impossible if the young are raised to be passive consumers of their society's military mentality." –War Resisters League

Toys ARE us!
A parent's perspective
The door before me opened soundlessly. But as I walked down the entrance hall, colors on the wall – geometrical patterns in vivid, angry colors – screamed at my senses. I rounded the corner to the display area and was completely overwhelmed by floor-to-ceiling shelves spilling over with merchandise for children. This was Toyland!

My initial shock at the raucous enormity of the place was soon accompanied by nostalgia as I walked those aisles, remembering with pleasure and pain, times when decisions about toys were an important part of my life, when the pull between our children's programmed wants and our value-oriented perspective on their needs were often in conflict.

Certainly, my husband and I were not always successful in providing creative substitutes when we, with studied deliberation, questioned our children's wants. Specific toys were important cultural symbols in their world, and it was difficult to explain why we rejected those symbols. My brief visit to a modern toy store convinced me that today's parents of young children face an even more difficult task. Giant shelves stocked with violent dolls and grotesque monsters – along with perfect imitations of military and police weapons – included every imaginable accessory for creative destruction.

Those symbols of violence – even scaled-down versions – gave off an oppressive, almost hallucinatory atmosphere. Children became "hyper" as soon as they entered the so-called "super action heroes" section. Their shrill screams of excitement could be heard throughout the store. Adults were affected, too. One mother walked up and down the aisles in a distraught state, lamenting loudly to anyone who would listen, "There's not a single puppet in the store! Can you believe it? Not a single puppet in the entire store!" That woman's anguished cry was real. And as I looked around me, her distress became mine. I realized that the absence of simple, creative playthings in that great toy depository is not accidental. It is a fact that speaks with authority about today's world.

It is a lamentable truth that we feel surrounded by violence; we live in an atmosphere that not only tolerates but encourages violence. In television programming, movies, and the print media – as well as current interpretations of America's role in the world – adults are surrounded by unspoken macho ideals such as "might makes right" and "survival of the fittest," supported with military might. We are encouraged in insidious ways to deal with weakness in other people and with other countries from a position of strength and always with "our best interest" in mind.

It is alarming, but not surprising, how these ideas of power and domination have penetrated our children's world. As participants in those values, toy industries believe that self-interest dictates both their role to provide and their right to sell violent toys. And their profit indicators support their good business decisions. Since 1982, the sale of war toys has risen more than 500 percent! Adults must face the fact that it is not children who supply the toy industry with their profit margins, it is adults who buy for children.

Also, adults may be contributing to the violence factor for today's children by providing another disturbing wrinkle to this complicated mixture of children, toys, and war games. It is possible that children who play violent war games are not simply victims of television advertising and an unscrupulous toy market. They also may be imitating adults with whom they live. This new phenomenon, The National Survival Game, is a complicated adult version of a child's game often referred to as Capture the Flag. Wearing camouflage trousers, jackets, gloves, heavy boots, and often using face-masks, these weekend war-game players carry

pistols whose pellets sting and raise welts, making it necessary to wear goggles. Players confess to getting hooked on the "adrenalin high" and "instinct toning" of a three-hour game, and many of them claim they have never felt so alive.

What does this mean? An admittedly simplistic analysis of these activities suggests that our society encourages adults to play like children and children to play like adults, with both groups using war games as a means for having fun. And on another level, national and international leaders also play at war with deadly games of "I dare you," in which nuclear holocaust – rather than the enemy's flag – is the prize of battle.

It may be a drastic leap in logic from the danger of war toys for our children to the specter of a nuclear holocaust. Unfortunately, the connection between the two may be more real than we want to believe. Today's adults and children are caught up in games that are far more frightening than those provided by the contents of shelves in a toy store. We have bought into our world leaders' obsessions with military solutions to people's problems.

And if we believe, with most child psychologists, that play is a child's work, we make our legacy to future generations when we decide to provide our children with up-to-date symbols of war. The values of our truculent, embattled society will become the norm for our children.

What can we do? To use words that come directly from war terminology, we can protect our children by providing them with a buffer zone – a "game against war" to which every thoughtful adult should be committed. But this means taking risks. We will certainly encounter the displeasure of our children if we interrupt their involvement with the symbols of their world. Even more than adults, children have difficulty trying to distance themselves from their culture. They are highly impressionable and easily conditioned to want what their friends have or what they see on television. Children who are allowed unrestricted exposure to mass-media hard sell – calculatingly and carefully designed by well-planned market research – are unlikely to want anything other than what they are told to want. Adults must assume some responsibility in determining when children's wants conflict with their needs.

Jesus once asked a question that may shed some light on this current dilemma with children. "Which one of you, if your child asks for bread, would give a stone? Or if he asks for a fish, would give him a scorpion?" We know the answer: no loving adult would feed a hungry child on a diet of stones and scorpions. But what is a parent to do if a child asks for a Voltron, a Gobot, or a Rambo doll? We believe that responsible, loving parents will refuse to feed a child's hunger for play on a diet of violence and savagery.

Each Christmas we are faced with questions about gift-giving. What do we give our children? What is appropriate for celebrating the birthday of the Prince of Peace? With that as a point of reference, some disciplined thinking about creative substitutes for violent toys is certainly in order.

What can we do?

It is unfortunate that corporate promoters find an easy target in children. Media hype and peer pressure make it almost impossible for children to prefer toys which promote reason, exploration, and sharing over toys that promote violence.

What is a caring parent or adult friend to do? Begin by carefully evaluating toys you buy. Every time you purchase a toy, your adult values are passed on to the child who receives that toy. Avoid buying toys that promote violence.

6. Would I feel comfortable involved in the child's play with this toy?

7. Are the concepts presented by the toy appropriate for a child?

8. What values does the toy promote? Does it promote concern for the earth? Is it in tune with what I want my child to grow up to be? (Questions from "Peace Through Tyranny," by Mary Pliska.)

Guidelines for selecting toys

1. Look the toy over carefully and think about its purpose. What will the child be learning or imitating from the use of this toy?

2. Read the packaging. What is the attitude toward life promoted by this toy?

3. What is the toy's play value? Can it be used again and again in a variety of ways? Is it appropriate for this child's age level? Will it isolate the child in play or assist the child in social development?

4. Does it help the child to develop imagination without being lost in a world of overwhelming fantasy?

5. Does it assist the child in learning to cope with and bring order to the real world?

Family activities

1. Talk with family members about attitudes and feelings toward war toys and offer suggestions for alternative toys and games.

2. Refuse to buy war toys for others and learn how to gracefully give them back when you receive them.

3. Ask other children not to bring war toys into your home.

4. Make up a television viewing schedule that eliminates violent shows or shows sponsored by war toy companies.

5. Create "No War Toys Zones" in your home, church, school.

6. Talk about what really happens in war. People are hurt and killed. Games, television shows and movies using guns seldom show the

real effect of what violence does to people.

7. Discuss the problems of war toys with all family members present. If the father or male caregiver is not present at the family discussion, the family receives an unspoken message that peace is a woman's role and war is a man's role.

8. Learn to play games which are nonviolent, active, and fun. The New Games book series is an excellent resource. Contact Alternatives for resources.

9. Spend time as a family in helping and caring for others in the community.

10. Role play how children might respond when invited by friends to play war games.

11. Draft a family letter to war toy manufacturers, cartoon producers and others who promote militarism to children. Tell them why you oppose what they do.

12. Encourage clergy, teachers and others in your community to address the topic of war toys and inform others of the adverse effects such toys may have on children.

(Family activities are from the brochure, "Toys Are for Fun: Not Fighting," produced by The Peace Resource Center, Des Moines, Iowa, 515/255-7114.)

I'm Dreaming of a Green Christmas

Miriam Youngquist-Thurow

*Miriam Youngquist-Thurow is the Program Coordinator for
Lutheran Outdoor Ministries, Fuquay-Varina, NC,
focusing on environmental education.*

As Christmas comes our way once more, it's difficult not to succumb to the advertising and hype enticing us to buy, buy, buy! Most of us spend as much as 70 percent of our discretionary income in November and December. Christmas accounts for more than a fifth of retail sales and two-fifths of store profits. These figures don't even begin to acknowledge the outrageous amount of waste produced by the biggest shopping binge of the year. Come December 26th, needle-bare Christmas trees, bags of crushed wrapping paper and discarded gift packaging sit in mounds at curbside. The production of gifts, decorations, party supplies, as well as travel for shopping and visiting place an even greater burden on our environment and its natural resources.

While gift-giving, decorating and celebrating together is often fun, we must keep in focus the reason behind our celebration: the joyous response to the greatest gift God gave to us, Jesus Christ. With that in mind, we could guess Jesus would be pleased if we honored his birthday and showed consideration for creation at the same time.

The following ideas will help to make your Christmas "green." Many of the ideas will be familiar, coming from traditions of days past; others may be new. Put a check next to the ones you will do. When you use even one alternative to the spending, consumptive mania, you will be taking a step toward greening up the Christmas season.

Decorations

North Americans cut over 35 million Christmas trees every year. We decorate our Christmas trees, our homes and our yards with countless strands of lights. We buy packaged tinsel which we discard soon after the holidays are over. While we might be able to spout off the cost of a pre-cut, six-foot Christmas tree and the price of a light-up ornament, we seldom consider the costs to the environment. What resources are used to produce our decorations? Where are hazardous production wastes disposed? How much valuable electricity do our lights use? What happens to the tree, tinsel, and empty cans of imitation snow after they leave our curb? Consider the following earth-friendly decorating tips.

Christmas tree

- Consider purchasing a live tree that can be planted in the yard. (In northern climates, it helps to dig the hole before the ground freezes.) Ask a local nursery or the Cooperative Extension Service for information on native trees, care and planting.
- Use an artificial tree. Even though it may seem "unnatural," you save the life of a tree every time you use it. (Purchase a well-made artificial tree that will last for years as the manufacture of plastic trees causes toxic pollution.)
- If you buy a cut tree, recycle it after the holidays. Place it near a bird feeder where birds can use it as cover. Or use dried branches and needles for mulch or compost and use the trunk for firewood. (Don't burn branches as the resins can cause chimney fires.) Find out if a local nature center needs wood chips for trails and ask if they have a chipper. Call a nursery or local solid waste removal service to find out who is recycling trees in your area.
- Use bits of nature to hang on the tree: pine cones, acorns, shells, dried flowers, unique small sticks or driftwood, etc.
- Use discarded toys, scrap materials, cardboard, bits of ribbon and some imagination to create a myriad of ornaments.
- Make dough ornaments: Use 4 cups flour, 1 cup salt, 1.5 cups water, and food coloring. Mix everything together and roll out with a rolling pin.

Use a knife, cookie cutters or container lids to make shapes. Press an ornament hook or loop of string into the dough for hanging. Bake at 150 degrees until shapes become hard. Paint the ornaments, if you wish.

- Use dried grasses or milkweed fluff from dry pods as a tinsel substitute. (Don't open milkweed pods until ready to decorate.) Use reusable glass icicles.
- Other

Indoors

- Make compostable wreaths. Dried fruits and vegetables make colorful additions to vine or evergreen wreaths. (Use a wire hanger to shape.) You can also use bits of nature: acorns or other nuts, dried leaves, pine cones, shells, sand dollars, dried flowers.
- Use the front of old Christmas cards to decorate walls and doorways.
- Use paper or cardboard to make Christian symbols to hang in windows or about the house. Make snowflakes out of construction paper or crochet some.
- Other

Outdoors

- Decorate outside trees with things the birds and squirrels will enjoy: popcorn and cranberry strings; pine cones covered with a peanut butter/corn meal mixture (plain peanut butter can cause birds to choke); corn-on-the-cob or cracked corn.
- Other

"Green" gifts

With a little energy and thought, we can give gifts that respect the receiver and creation. Expensive store-bought gifts with excessive packaging not only cost the buyer a lot, they also cost our environment. And when we go hunting from store to store for that "perfect" gift, we use gallons and gallons of gasoline; each gallon of gasoline we use releases harmful emissions into the atmosphere. By making gifts, carefully selecting purchased gifts, and using creative gift-wrap, we can make our Christmas giving more "green." Here are some ideas.

Make gifts

- Construct building blocks from lumberyard scraps. Cut, sand, and paint if desired.

- Sew some durable, reusable grocery bags from heavy material.
- Cover boxes with fabric for various uses: big boxes for toys down to little boxes for jewelry or odds and ends.
- Make cloth napkins out of absorbent and stain-camouflaging fabric.
- Design a calendar with favorite photos or children's artwork.
- Give plants in hand-decorated pots.
- Fill a basket with wildflower seeds or vegetable seeds.
- Build a birdhouse or bird feeder. Make up your own design or get plans from a nature center, library or bookstore. You might even give a supply of birdseed.
- Give jelly, cookies, or one of your holiday food specialties. Pack in reusable jars or tins.
- Consider other talents you have to give.
- Other

When buying gifts
- Buy gifts that the recipient really needs. Don't buy gifts targeted to "the person who has everything."
- Choose gifts that promote awareness of environmental issues and encourage action.
- Consider how a gift is packaged: Is the packaging recyclable? Is it biodegradable? Is it excessive?
- Consider the materials the gift is made of and how it was produced.
- Give gifts made by Third-World crafts people.
- Avoid buying gifts which require the use of electricity, gasoline or batteries.
- Other

Gift wrapping
- Buy recycled wrapping paper.
- Save the comics and use them, or even the regular newsprint.
- Use the fronts of old Christmas cards for decorative touches or name tags.
- Use tissue paper and decorate with a festive stamp and ink. You can make a stamp by carving a potato.
- Wrap gifts with old maps.
- Use cloth napkins or scarves.
- Wrap a gift in a pillow case, a decorative towel, a t-shirt, a mitten, etc. (The wrapping can be part of the gift.)
- Replace bows with evergreens, dried or silk flowers, snowflake cutouts, berries, paper cranes, etc.
- Other

Events

Family and community gatherings during the holidays are an important and fulfilling part of our Christmas celebrations. Sometimes, though, we get carried away and plan elaborate affairs that take a toll on our budgets, our environment and our spirits. Consider these ideas to create joyful "green" celebrations.

Outings

- Plan a family outing that doesn't involve shopping. Go hiking at a nearby nature center or park. Go ice skating, sledding, biking, bowling, horseback riding, etc.
- Check with nearby camps, State or Provincial Parks, or nature organizations to find out about and take part in events they have planned.
- Volunteer to plant trees in poor urban areas or parks. If weather is too cold, make arrangements to volunteer in the spring.
- Organize a group to pick up trash in your neighborhood.
- Other

Entertaining at home

- Turn down the thermostat to conserve fuel.
- Use regular dishes and cloth napkins instead of paper throw-away products.
- Buy snack items in the largest possible size to cut down on packaging waste.
- Other

These suggestions are merely a springboard for ideas you and your family can develop. Consider other ways you can bring the full meaning of Christmas to your family while doing God's creation a service at the same time.

"Those Little Envelopes Seemed Small"

Kathie Klein

*Kathie Klein, Alternatives' former Art Director,
lives in Atlanta with her husband and sons.*

A small package rests in front of you. Slowly you begin to open it, savoring the mystery and expectation. What is it? A watch could fit in that box. A nice little piece of art glass could, too. The paper falls beside you. You lift the cover and remove a small scroll of paper tied with a ribbon. It could be a gift certificate. You spend it five times in the next instant as your fingers untie the ribbon and begin to unroll the little paper. A sweater, a CD, a cordless drill, shoes, dinner out …. You read the paper: "A donation has been made in your name to Save the Whales. Merry Christmas from Bill and Tina." Your heart sinks as music from that new CD fades in your mind.

Many of us have imagined just such a scene as we consider giving and receiving "alternative" gifts, whether donations or other kinds of unusual gifts. On the giving side, we don't trust that an alternative gift will bring pleasure to the recipient. On the receiving side, we sometimes find our own greed crowding out the joy and connection of sharing with others.

What can we do about our concern that a recipient won't find pleasure in our gift, or won't think it's an acceptable one? Planning such gifts takes some discretion and careful consideration. Some people we know would happily receive a donation made in their name. One woman told me she loved it when people made donations for her, because it allowed her to stretch her own charitable dollar even further. Some people have never seriously considered such a gift, but might like the idea if we talked with them about it.

If we lack confidence in our gift selections for some people, the idea of an alternative gift might be an opportunity to change an awkward situation. Some older people who are trying to clear out a lifetime of accumulation might see a donation made in their name as support for their current task. Some people might prefer to be surprised by a donation, others might like to be consulted in choosing an organization or project to receive the donation. Some families will be able to adopt a new mode of giving *en masse*, for others it will happen on an individually negotiated basis.

It can be a difficult task to change our giving patterns. There can be some discomfort and disappointment. Years ago, two parents decided to make donations as Christmas gifts to their high school age children. The family talked together and each child chose an organization. However, on Christmas day, as the father said, "It went over like a lead balloon." The mother said, "Those little envelopes hanging on the tree seemed small."

How can we address the discomfort of a struggle between our altruism and our personal greed? Recognizing and acknowledging the discomfort is important in itself. The disappointment we fear in others is sometimes a mirror of the disappointment we ourselves would feel at not getting a "real present," a "something." In recognizing and naming our own greed we can question it for information about ourselves, confess it and seek to grow.

After years of exploring different ways of giving, the family mentioned above has made alternative giving an important part of their celebration. At Christmas, the mother – who had had cataract surgery earlier in the year – was deeply touched to receive this card from her daughter and son-in-law: "To wish you a joyous Christmas, a gift of one eye surgery in Ghana has been sent in your honor to God's family in need, so that sick, hungry and homeless people can find new hope to help themselves and so that our global village can experience a new day of peace."

The path of alternative giving can lead from "our" trees, "our" gifts, "our" own, to our great extended family, our brothers and sisters in the global village.

In the Spirit of Saint Nicholas

Mike and Kathe Sherer

Mike Sherer is a Lutheran pastor who serves as editor of the Metro Lutheran.
Kathe Sherer is a registered nurse and homemaker.
Now living in the Twin Cities, the Sherers began celebrating Christmas
without Santa Claus in 1972, when their children were toddlers.

When the two of us were children, we eagerly looked forward to the coming of the jolly old man in the red suit. Even though both of us were raised in families where resources were limited, Santa Claus still came and none in either of our families was ever forgotten.

Somewhere along the way to establishing our own family, however, something changed. Our culture moved more and more into consumerism. Fewer of us wanted for anything. The electronic media, increasingly effective advertising motivators, became pervasive.

We didn't like the trends in which we found ourselves becoming immersed. Voices from the marketplace coaxed us to buy and buy more and more, especially during a season

we had been raised to believe was God's special time. It seemed to us that gifts exchanged at Christmas were becoming a distraction from the meaning of God's best gift. We were painfully aware that many in our society were left out, individuals who were more in need than those to whom we gave Christmas presents (and more in need than those whom Santa came to visit).

Good-bye Santa, hello Saint Nicholas

Upon researching Christmas and Santa, we made an unexpected discovery. We had thought we would find that Santa had his origins in pagan mythology somewhere in the distant past. Instead, the trail led us back to the fourth century, to an actual Christian pastor, the Bishop of Myra.

Bishop Nicholas, we discovered, was a kind man who cared for the people not only in his congregation but in the wider community. He began to link up those people with an excess of material goods with those who had too little. But Nicholas did it in a surprising way: he maintained a double-blind. In other words, the giver never knew who received the gift and the recipient never knew who gave it. This marvelous arrangement made it possible for people to escape the conditions usually attached to gifts.

Bishop Nicholas' reputation lived long after him. However, through the centuries his story was confused with legend and mythology. By the 1800s, the saintly, generous Christian pastor had been transformed into a jolly, bearded man in a red suit who came to give gifts to well-behaved children. The legacy had been betrayed.

Therefore, when our daughters Heidi and Wendy were young, we decided to begin a new tradition. We simply did not invite Santa Claus into our Christmas observance. We did all the other things that Christians ordinarily do in December: we put up a tree in our home and decorated it (without the gifts beneath, however); we celebrated the season with special foods; we played the music of the season; we worshipped God on Christmas Eve and (when we could find a service) on Christmas morning.

Gifts that really matter

We decided to try to recapture the spirit of Bishop Nicholas. We began to celebrate his feast day, December 6th. Our daughters created a simple puppet show which told the story of Nicholas. In addition, we took the money we would have spent on Christmas presents, and instead, gave it (anonymously, in the Nicholas spirit) to a person or ministry in great need of our help. Our daughters helped by creating original Saint Nicholas cards to be sent with the check.

Where did the money go?

- One year, a local kindergarten teacher had a student in her class whose family was in need of socks and underwear. We purchased and wrapped these items and she delivered them to the family.

- Some years, we gave to a ministry agency which helped unwed mothers take care of their young children.
- In recent years, we have sent our Nicholas gift to a project which sends easy-to-operate-and-maintain garden tractors to farmers in the third world.
- Lately we are sending our gift to a ministry which helps the homeless secure housing for themselves.

How our children responded

We had some real misgivings about removing Santa Claus from our Christmas celebration and inviting Saint Nicholas in. We were concerned about the effects the changes would have on our daughters. We had no doubt there would be a good and healthy result, because we were offering them an alternative that was built on a Christian value system rather than on marketplace persuasion. But we knew that our daughters would face a lot of pressure from peers as they grew older, and probably even some ridicule.

There were some difficulties. One of the most unexpected sources of confusion and confrontation was from relatives. Since we didn't know

how else to escape the exchange mentality we thought we were caught up in, we decided to make a clean break with Christmas gift-giving. After we stopped giving Christmas gifts to relatives, we imagined that they would stop giving to our family as well. Some did, but some insisted they wanted to continue. They said, "Think of what you're doing to your children. You are robbing them of the spirit of giving."

Our reply was, "We intend to give gifts to our children on their birthdays and at other times of the year. We simply want to keep this special season and our celebration free from too much materialism." In time most of our relatives accepted this idea and honored our request. A few never quite made it that far, but we knew they respected what we were trying to do.

In school, both Heidi and Wendy had to deal with the fact that all during December and early January other children would talk – on the playground, at the bus stop, in the lunch line – about "what I want for Christmas ... what I'm getting for Christmas ... what I got for Christmas." Our older daughter came home from school one day and reported this conversation:

"What are you getting for Christmas?"

"Nothing. Christmas is Jesus' birthday, not mine."

"Oh, I feel sorry for you. You're not getting *anything* for Christmas!"

"Well, I feel sorry for *you* if that's all you think Christmas is about."

Our younger daughter had similar experiences. Once her class held a Christmas gift exchange during December. The gifts were distributed by using a modified version of musical chairs. When she told the teacher that her family did not practice Christmas gift exchanges, she was given a special opportunity: she started and stopped the music as the others in her class "exchanged gifts" with one another. When discussing the experience at home afterwards, we learned that she really felt good about having been able to speak out for her family's special custom, and for not having participated in something that did not make sense to her.

Heidi and Wendy are now in college. We have long ago put the stocking puppets away in a shoe box, but the spirit of Nicholas giving contin-

ues. From time to time, especially as December approaches, we sometimes talk about the fact that we raised our daughters to be "different" than their peers. Sometimes we have wondered whether they resented or regretted the experience, and whether they will want to continue the practice in the homes they might one day establish.

When asked, both have replied similarly: they said that celebrating Saint Nicholas Day and Christmas as we did has given special meaning to the season. They both expressed a desire to follow a similar practice in their homes.

Real benefits

It's been great to be able to ignore the newspaper and television advertising from Thanksgiving to Christmas each year, knowing that there will be no "Christmas shopping rush" at our house. When others ask one of us, as someone always does during this normally hectic season, "Have you got your Christmas shopping done yet?" we have a natural opportunity to talk about an alternative that works. In many cases the surprised listener concludes the conversation by saying, "Say, that's really something! Could you give me a copy of the article that describes what you do?" We're always happy to oblige.

For us, Christmas is no longer a frantic, but rather a holy, peaceful and enriching time. And we have the assurance that, rather than spending too much on those who do not need it, through our family's gifts we are helping those who do.

What To Tell the Folks

What will our extended family and friends say if we want to change some of the ways we give at Christmas? The following is an excerpt from an actual letter one couple sent to their family and friends. It may give you some ideas for what you might want to say.

Dear Family:

Over the past few years, we have discovered that Christmas has become a time to "get through" rather than a time to savor and appreciate. Perhaps our expanding family has contributed to making the get-ready time more frenzied than it was in the past.

Of course, the seasonal contacts with all of you – whether by telephone, in person, or through an exchange of gifts – always brings us joy. When the season comes to a close, though, we can't help but wonder if our mode of celebration pleases God and reflects the real significance of Christmas.

In most cases, none of us is truly in need of material things, but our spiritual lives may be less full than they could be. One way to enrich our spiritual lives is to extend a helping hand to others. As your gift to us in this coming Christmas, would you consider making a gift of your time, your talent, or your money to someone or some group in need? The only request we make is that you tell us about the gift you have given. In return, we propose to make a similar gift to you. We would welcome your thought on what we might give which would be meaningful to you.

We recognize that there is something special in sharing tangible gifts. Therefore, along with sharing with those in need, we think exchanging inexpensive purchased items or products of our own labor is appropriate and certainly within the spirit of Christmas. And, of course, young children may not appreciate the significance of our suggested approach and, therefore, should not have to participate.

Please think about the subject for a while and let us have your reactions and suggestions. We want to know what you think, even if you've completed your shopping!

We love you all dearly and will respect whatever you decide to do. Our major concern is that we refocus our efforts toward a more meaningful celebration of the birth of Jesus Christ.

Simple Christmas Ideas for Kids

A Sense of Wonder

With their boundless enthusiasm and sense of wonder, children make the Christmas season extra-special. If you think that only finding the hottest toys on the market under the tree will make your kids happy, think again. Children are often fascinated by the simplest things life has to offer. We've all heard of the child who found the cardboard box her present came in more interesting than the new toy itself!

Here are a few fun ideas to involve your children in Christmas preparation and celebration.

Paper Cranes

Paper cranes have become a symbol of peace and hope. (See the story of the Japanese girl, Sadako, on page 148.) The paper cranes will make beautiful and symbolic Christmas tree ornaments.

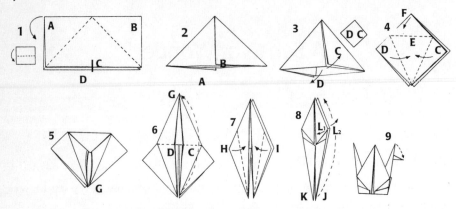

How to fold a paper crane:

1. Fold a *square* piece of lightweight paper in half horizontally. Then fold A back to bottom center (D), and B *forward* to front bottom center (C).

2. Your paper should look like this.

3. Pull C (the front) and D (the back) apart all the way until you have a flat diamond (as in small diagram).

4. Fold top layers of C and D inward to center line E and fold down F along dotted line.

5. Your paper should look like this.

6. Now unfold step 4. Take top layer *only* at G and pull it up, making use of the crease (dotted line). This allows points C and D to fold back to the center line along the creases. Turn paper over and repeat steps 4, 5, and 6, ignoring new flap topped by point G.

7. With split at bottom, fold H and I inward so that the edges meet the center line. Turn paper over and repeat.

8. Temporarily open flaps at L_1 and L_2. Pull J up to top *between* flaps and close flaps (L_1 and L_2). Repeat with K. Fold down head. Fold down wings.

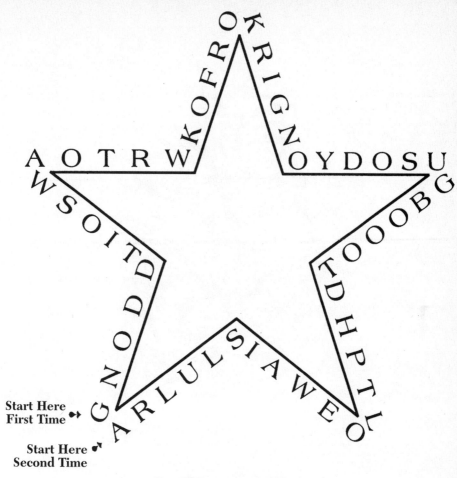

Start Here First Time ➤

Start Here Second Time ➤

Follow the Star

Go around the star twice, clockwise. Write down every other letter.

"G __ __   __ __   __ __   __ __ __ __

__ __   __ __ __,   __ __ __ __   __ __

__ __ __ __   __ __ __   __ __

__ __ __   __ __ __,__   __ __ __ __

__ __ __ __ __ __ __ __   **E.**"

Philippians 2:13

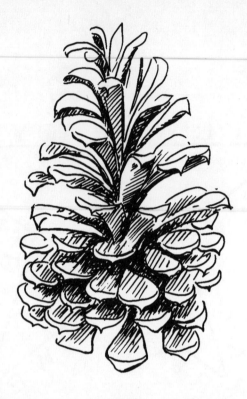

Decorate Inside and Out

Make pinecone treats for the birds this Christmas. Gather or purchase pinecones. Mix together peanut butter and corn meal. (Plain peanut butter can cause birds to choke.) Spread the pinecones with the mixture. Then roll the pinecones in birdseed or cracked corn. Place them in the branches of trees or shrubs or other places birds can find them.

Be in touch with nature this season by bringing a little of the outdoors inside. Decorate some pinecones with scraps of lace, bits of ribbon, small shells or dried flowers. Try covering the pinecones in glue and rolling them in some of the leftover birdseed.

A Special Birthday Gift

Finish the message by putting the letters from the boxes in order on the lines provided below. Start with the letter in box number 1. Then find the letter for box number 2 and so on. Your last letter will be the one in box 42.

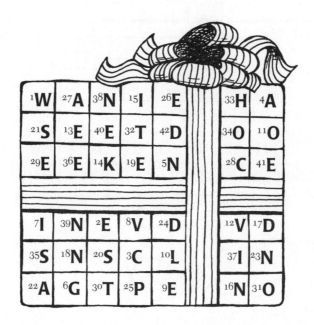

¹W	²⁷A	³⁸N	¹⁵I	²⁶E		³³H	⁴A
²¹S	¹³E	⁴⁰E	³²T	⁴²D		³⁴O	¹¹O
²⁹E	³⁶E	¹⁴K	¹⁹E	⁵N		²⁸C	⁴¹E
⁷I	³⁹N	²E	⁸V	²⁴D		¹²V	¹⁷D
³⁵S	¹⁸N	²⁰S	³C	¹⁰L		³⁷I	²³N
²²A	⁶G	³⁰T	²⁵P	⁹E		¹⁶N	³¹O

As a birthday gift to Jesus,

— —   — — —   — — — —

— — — —,   — — — — — — — —

— — —   — — — — — —   — — —

— — — — —   — —   — — — — .

The Spirit of Christmas

Finish the message by putting the letters from the boxes in order on the lines provided below. Start with the letter in box number 1. Then find the letter for box number 2 and so on. Your last letter will be the one in box number 47.

¹S

²⁹I | ¹⁰T

³A | ³⁹R | ²¹R

²³A | ¹³H | ³²H | ¹⁶E

³⁴N | ¹⁷W | ²⁶N | ⁶N | ³⁷Y

⁸W | ⁴³E | ²⁸S | ⁴⁵E | ²²E | ¹⁴O

³⁶R | ⁴⁰H | ¹²T | ³¹K | ⁴⁷S | ⁹I | ³⁰C

¹⁸H | ⁴R | ²⁵O | ⁴¹O | ⁴⁶S | ⁷G | ²⁴L | ⁴²M

²⁷E | ⁴⁴L | ³³U | ¹⁵S | ³⁵G | ²⁰A | ³⁸O | ¹¹H | ²H

⁵I

¹⁹O

The way you can keep the spirit of Christmas with you the whole year is by

— — — — — — — — — — — — —

— — — — — — — — — — — — —

— — — — — —, — — — — —, — — — — — — —

— — — — — — — — — — —.

Christmas Can Get Confusing ...

Instructions: Starting at the middle, try to find your way out of the maze.

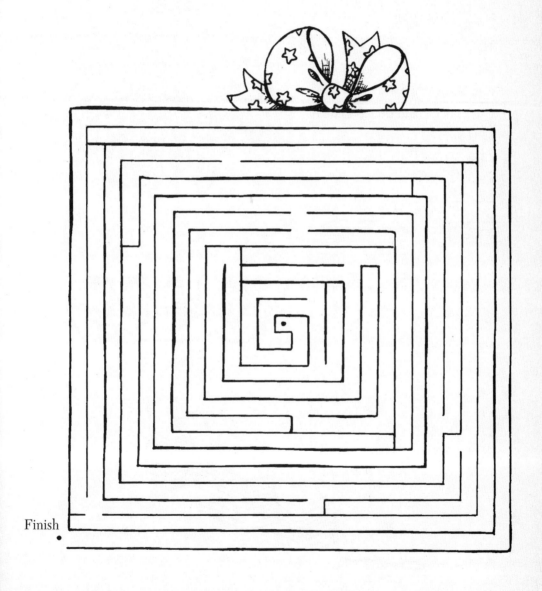

Finish

Make Paper Stars this Christmas

German paper stars are often made from gold or silver foil or metallic paper or red paper. Use a strip of paper 22" long and 3" wide.

1. Make 3/4" accordion fold over a block
2. Cut. You might use a utility kife
3. Use a needle and thread to tie one end together
4. Glue or tape

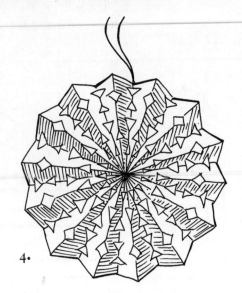

4.

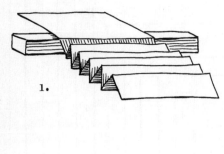

1.

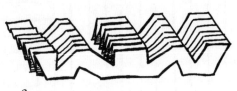

2.

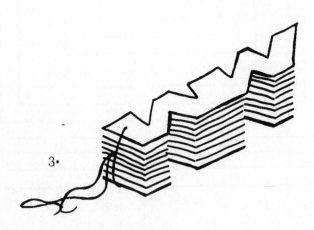

3.

A Holiday Star ...

Photocopy the picture of the star (below) on white or colored paper. Cut out along the dotted line. Fold in half at points as indicated. Then using a needle and thread, pull knotted thread up through the center, and back down to create a loop. Tie off end of thread. Hang on your tree or another special place.

A Jesse Tree

Many meaningful Christian symbols help us focus on preparation for Christmas during Advent ... the Advent wreath (Christian symbols for MC tree) and eventually the Christmas tree. When so many commercial symbols try to distract us from the real meaning of the season, the Jesse Tree is a lesser known but also powerful, visual focal point.

At the beginning of Advent (no later than four weeks prior to Christmas) cut a branch from a lilac or forsythia just above a bud and place it in a vase filled with water, make the cut clean and at an angle. A vase filled with clear glass beads and water will provide support for the Jesse Tree. Maintain a water level above the cut and the Jesse Tree will blossom by Christmas. Lilacs, regardless of their blossom color, will bloom white when forced this way.

At the end of chapter 10, Isaiah foretells the end of the Assyrian rule over Jerusalem as God "hack(ing) down the thickets of a forest with an ax." Razing it to stumps. The Israelites – David's line – had been so razed.

Then comes the promise in Isaiah 11:1-2, from which the Jesse Tree gets its name – "A shoot shall come out from the stump of Jesse, and a branch shall grow out of his roots."

And from that line will come the Messiah ... a new branch from a stump ... a branch stronger and more fruitful than the original tree.

The Jesse Tree is beautiful by itself, But it can also hold ornaments, symbols of the season of Advent, the season of waiting ... a scroll to remember the prophecies, ... a dove to remind us of the peace that comes with the Messiah ... a crown for David's son, Solomon ... a rose with twelve petals, one for each of Jesse's sons from whom sprang the twelve tribes of Israel. On the next pages some Jesse Tree Symbols are provided for you to use.

As we hang the ornaments – usually one per day – we tell the related story. The prophecies come to life with the appearance of blooms – new life from an old branch – as they did with the birth of Jesus Christ.

For more information about possible designs of the ornaments, contact your public or church library.

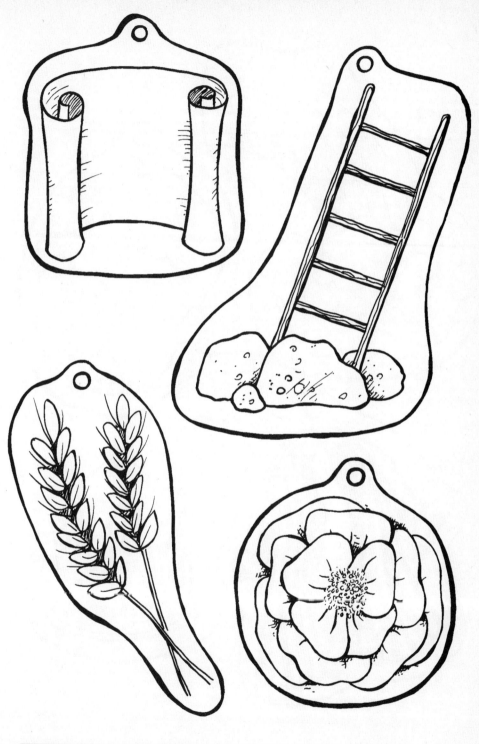

PART 2

Celebrate

Introduction

Discovering the Soul of Christmas

"Whose Birthday Is It, Anyway?"

The Story of Jason (Matthew 3:1)

Reverend Arley Fadness

Reverend Arley Fadness, author, publisher and pastor of Messiah Lutheran in North Mankato, MN, originally wrote the Story of Jason on December 7, 1980.

In the land of Puzzling Tales there lived an eight-year-old boy by the name of Jason.

Now in this land and in the neighborhood where Jason lived, the unexpected always happened.

Instead of football they played kneeball; instead of the children "going to school" the teachers were busy "going to homes." In the summer time it was not uncommon to see water freeze and in the winter time leaves grew on trees. It was a funny, strange place.

One incident in the land of Puzzling Tales stands out. When it was time for Jason's ninth birthday, as usual, the unusual happened.

Jason's grandparents came from their home across the state to help celebrate, but of course when they got to Jason's neighborhood they went immediately to the Browns down the street and visited and stayed there.

When Jason's mother baked the birthday cake she gave it to the Letter Carrier to eat.

And when all the neighborhood kids heard it was Jason's birthday they exchanged gifts with one another and of course, Jason got none.

There was a blizzard of birthday cards. The post office had to hire extra workers and work longer hours to handle the deluge of cards. Of course, in the land of Puzzling Tales the expected was the unexpected and all the kids, the moms and dads, grandparents, even a couple of dogs and a parakeet got cards, while poor Jason got none.

Finally about nine o'clock in a fit of frustration and anger Jason went out of his house, borrowed the school cheerleaders' megaphone, rode up and down the street on his unicycle and shouted at the top of his lungs,

"WHOSE BIRTHDAY IS IT, ANYWAY?"

And the night was so silent that all night long echoes bounced off the mountain sides: "Whose birthday is it, anyway?" "Whose birthday is it, anyway?"

The baby Jesus will be kidnapped again this year and held ransom for millions of dollars. This year North Americans will surrender about 20 billion dollars to the stores to buy gifts to swap.

But it is Jesus' birthday! Jesus ought to receive the gifts. Jesus said "Inasmuch as you have done it to the least of these, you have done it to me." We give to Jesus when we give to the poor, the weak, the hungry, the homeless, the refugees, the prisoners.

It will be a great birthday celebration when God's people begin in earnest to give once again to Jesus. For after all, it is his birthday, isn't it?

Readings, Reflections and Activities

In the following section you will find three sets of biblical readings, as well as reflections and activities designed for use by individuals, families, or other groups. (Each set of reflections also contains an Advent calendar. With slight modification, these calendars can be used any year.)

The selection of readings and their grouping has been done according to the *Revised Common Lectionary*. (A lectionary is a collection of readings from scripture which the church uses as part of its communal worship. The schedule of readings follows the church calendar and is organized according to a repeating, three-year cycle – thus the three sets of readings included in this volume. The years of the cycle are simply designated as Year A, Year B, and Year C. Note that the readings in this book begin with Year C, as that is the lectionary year for 1997.)

The organization of the readings and reflections in this book according to the lectionary is for the convenience of those who may wish to use this book in conjunction with or in addition to their participation in church celebrations and worship, where the specific lectionary readings may be used.

All readers, but especially those who do not participate in church celebrations, should feel free to use whichever set of readings and reflections appeals to them most.

Making an Advent Wreath

Many people who participate in the kind of meditative or devotional practice contained in this book combine them with the use of an Advent wreath during the four weeks prior to Christmas. Although some of the activities provided in this book specifically suggest the use of an Advent wreath and others do not, you may wish to make it part of your celebrations regardless of which set of meditations you choose to use.

The tradition of using an Advent wreath and its candles to set apart the Sundays of the season comes from early in the history of the church. Traditionally, it is a holly and evergreen garland, holding four small candles and one large central candle. The four small candles are usually purple, the color of Advent that reminds us of repentance and preparation. The large candle is either red or white, symbolizing Christ. The evergreen branches placed around the candles remind us of God's unending love.

On the first Sunday of Advent (the fourth Sunday prior to Christmas day), light one of the small candles and then read the scripture selections and meditation for that day, reflecting on the day's significance. On each of the subsequent Sundays prior to Christmas, light an additional candle during your time of meditation. On Christmas day, in addition to the four small candles, you will also light the large center candle – the Christ candle.

The Advent wreath can be constructed in any number of ways with a variety of materials. Here is one way:

1. Take a large flat shallow bowl (at least nine inches in diameter) and fill it with sand or coarse salt.

2. Place the four purple candles around the outside with the large candle in the center. Stick them down into the sand or salt so that they are placed securely.

3. Make a circle of evergreens and place them around the bowl.

4. Place the wreath and candles in a prominent place (at the center of the table, on a mantel, etc.) where they can stay through Christmas.

Advent and Christmas Calendars

Without calendars, there's no telling how disorganized our lives would be. Calendars add the structure that binds together day-to-day living. The school calendar is one example. In late August or early September the new school year begins and summer vacation is over. To help students get ready to start a new school year, we have created periods of orientation. When June arrives, schooling comes to an end. We celebrate this event with ceremonies of graduation or (hopefully) promotion.

Our churches have also created calendars to guide and teach us in the mysteries of our faith. Within these calendars there are holidays or feasts for celebrating important events. In addition, periods of orientation help us prepare for and to understand the importance of these events.

Christmas Day has been part of Christian calendars for more than 16 centuries. Each year a billion people stop what they are doing to remember the birth of Jesus. Christmas is celebrated on every continent and on islands in every ocean around the world.

Advent

Advent, too, is part of the Christmas calendar, not as a holiday or feast but as a time of preparation. In a sense, it is our orientation into the Christmas season. We often feel frustrated over how commercialized Christmas has become. Advent offers us time to de-commercialize our lives. By observing Advent we can actively make and follow the plans needed to orient our households and our lives toward the One whose birthday we will celebrate.

Advent begins on the Sunday nearest November 30 and includes the four Sundays before Christmas. No one knows for sure when Advent was first observed. It appears that fifth century Gaul (now France, Belgium and Luxembourg) was the place of its origin. It also seems likely that Advent was modeled after Lent. Advent, then, is more a time of thoughtful repentance than it is "that time allotted us to get our Christmas shopping done."

Advent has two purposes: to prepare us for celebrating the birth of Jesus and to make us look ahead to the second coming. Advent is a season that can draw upon both our practical abilities to plan and make ready and also upon our imagination as we think to the future.

Christmas

In much of North America, Christmas ends as soon as the dinner dishes are cleared. We have come to mark the end of Christmas by discarding things: the Christmas tree, table scraps and mountains of used wrapping paper. The post-Christmas season begins when we hit the shopping malls to return unwanted gifts or to take advantage of the numerous sales.

Traditionally, though, Christmas does not end on December 25th. The season of Christmas has twelve days and actually ends on Epiphany. Remember the carol, "On the twelfth day of Christmas, my true love gave to me ..." These extra days offer opportunities to learn about other events associated with Jesus' birth. By observing the entire Christmas season we can better understand what it means for Christ to be "living among us" (John 1:14).

Epiphany

While Mary, Joseph and the newly born Jesus were still in Bethlehem, they had a visit from a group of "wise men" or magi (Matthew 2:1-12). Through the centuries this event has come to signify the revealing of Jesus as messiah to the world. Epiphany (January 6th) is the day set aside to remember this visit. The name Epiphany has its root in the Greek word meaning to show. In North America this holiday (or feast) has become almost completely overshadowed by Christmas Day.

By seeing how Epiphany relates to Advent and Christmas day, we can better understand what it is all about. As was described earlier, part of the purpose of Advent is to help us get ready for what theologians call the "First Advent" (or the incarnation of God in Christ). And on Christmas Day we celebrate the birth of Jesus as the fulfillment of that promise. Then on Epiphany we celebrate God giving us a glimpse of who Jesus is: through the magi seeking the One whom the prophets spoke of.

What marks the close of the Christmas season is not the disposal of waste, but instead the celebration of the introduction of the Messiah to the world.

We have included three different Advent calendars in this book – one for each collection of readings, reflections, and activities. While the individual calendars are designated – Lectionary Cycle Year A (1998), B (1999), or C (1997), with a little adaptation they may be used any year.

Advent/Christmas Calendar

Lectionary Cycle Year C (1997)

Traveling to Bethlehem

Imagine, right now, all over our planet, people of every race and age are getting ready for Christmas. Just how are we to prepare ourselves for this great festival? What can we do to make our homes ready?

For 15 centuries, the thoughtful and quiet season of Advent has been there to help us make and follow the plans needed to orient our lives towards Bethlehem, and to prepare us for Jesus' victorious return.

In late 20th century North America the world around us at this time of year is a busy and chaotic place. For many people, the weeks before Christmas have turned into a dizzying frenzy of shopping, decorating, party-going and traveling. More than ever, we need to observe Advent. For some this will be a new experience; for others, it will be a time to re-experience all this season can truly be.

Through daily thoughts and actions, this Advent calendar helps us begin to experience the peace and joy the birth of Jesus brings.

November

30 Choose an organization you want to support this Christmas. Decorate a can to hold the money you collect while using this calendar.

December

1 Advent was originally a time of self-examination. Take a few moments to think about and write down three hopes you have for this Advent. Place your list along with the lists of other household members in a sealed envelope.

2 If you plan to decorate a tree this season, consider purchasing a live root tree. Have a tree planting ceremony for the new year to give thanks for the blessings of the season. (Ask your local nursery for planting tips.)

3 Read Jeremiah 33:16. Let family members ask for particular kinds of safety this season: from interrupting, from teasing, to hear words of love, to try something new. Make a family commitment.

December

4 Jesus is referred to by many names in the Bible: Emmanuel, Prince of Peace, etc. Make a list of the names you can think of and meditate on the significance of each one. Give five cents for each name on your list.

5 Think of those in your family and community who may find Christmas a difficult time – an elderly person, a single parent, an unemployed person, a person who has recently lost a loved one. Invite them for dinner or for coffee and cookies.

6 Some people exchange Christmas gifts today, St. Nicholas Day. How would this practice change the focus of the rest of the season? Could this tradition be used or adapted in your family next year? Talk it over.

7 Plan a meeting with those in your extended family to discuss Christmas giving. Or write a letter to your family outlining your ideas for alternative giving.

December

8 Make music a part of your Christmas celebrations. Organize or attend carol singing at church, in your neighborhood, at home. Give ten cents for every Christmas song you hear this week.

9 Spend some time with your family. Turn off the TV and play a favorite game. Bake cookies together. Read a story aloud.

10 Consider sending handmade Christmas cards. Gather your family and make one-of-a-kind greetings using construction paper, crayons, markers, glue, etc.

11 What gifts do you want this Christmas? Give ten cents for every non-material gift you hope to receive.

12 Today people in Mexico celebrate the festival of the Virgin of Guadalupe, a celebration popular with the poor and Native Americans. Learn more about this holiday.

December

13 Rearrange all the furniture in your living room until Christmas. Let it remind you of the need for change, for seeing with new eyes.

14 Today is St. Lucia Day. Lucia wore a crown of candles to light the way as she carried food to Christians hiding from their persecutors. Turn off the lights and light candles in the room. Pray for those who live in fear today.

15 Do you know the names of the people who collect your trash? Find out. Offer them a gift of baked goods or invite them to your Christmas party. Read Luke 14:12-14.

16 How can you bring good news to someone in need this week? What rough ways can you help smooth?

17 Learn about holiday food traditions in other countries. Try one out.

December

18 Read Philippians 1:3-11. Make a list of the people in your life for whom you are thankful. Give five cents for each name.

19 There is less than a week till Christmas. Do the elements of inner and outer preparation, anticipation and celebration seem balanced? Consider your goals and priorities for the rest of the week.

20 As you shop for Christmas foods, consider using cloth bags or reuse the bags from your last visit to the grocery store.

21 Are you welcoming visitors this holiday? Imagine them as magi coming to celebrate the birth of Christ. Imagine yourself as an innkeeper. Give 25 cents for every guest in your home this season.

22 Take some time to look through photographs of past Christmases. What do you see and remember? Choose one photo and share a favorite story that it brings to mind.

December

23 Russian legend tells of Baboushka, a woman who was too busy cooking and cleaning to journey with the magi to see baby Jesus. Set aside 30 minutes today to visit the Christ Child in your heart.

24 Open the envelope containing your lists of hopes for Advent. Think about or discuss with those in your household: How were my hopes realized this Advent? What would I do differently? Give 50 cents for each hope.

25 Imagine the nativity anew. "A baby with olive skin, dark eyes and curly black hair was born of Jewish parents in an impoverished Third World country. This Jewish child was born into slavery ... " (*Catholic Agitator,* Dec. 1991).

26 Read Acts 6-7. Today is Boxing Day, the day we remember St. Stephen, the first Christian martyr. Fill a box with food or clothing and give it to someone in need.

December

27 When have your neighbors been a blessing to you? Give ten cents for each situation you can remember.

28 Read Matthew 2:1-18. Where are children in danger today? Pray for the children of the world.

29 Remember the times when you have been sick this year. How did the people around you care for you? How can you care for those who are ill?

30 So often we take blessings for granted. As you go through the day, jot down things you are thankful for. At bedtime, offer a prayer of thanksgiving. Give five cents for each blessing.

31 A Spanish custom has people place each person's name in the "urn of fate." Two names are drawn at a time and each pair is best friends for the coming year. Draw names in your family and do a kind deed for your pal daily until Epiphany.

January

1 Give the gift of time. Teach a child to play a game from your childhood.

2 In some ways Christmas is fading, isn't it? Choose a part of Christmas to carry into this new year with you. Share your plans at dinner.

3 Look at the shoes in your closet. Consider the different kinds of journeys you undertake with each pair. Give 50 cents for each journey you can think of.

4 Epiphany approaches. Many years ago the magi journeyed toward the place where the Christ Child rested. Go outside and look at the night sky. Can you see any stars? Take a moment to think about what guides you toward Jesus today.

January

5 Look around you. What are your three most precious possessions? What would lead you to give those away?

6 On Epiphany, the magi brought Jesus gifts of gold, frankincense and myrrh. What gifts would Jesus want today? Give the money in your giving can to the organization you chose to support.

Michael Crosby

Let Us Go to Bethlehem

Lectionary Cycle C

Services by Mary Foulke; activities by Michelle McKinnon Buckles

Introduction

"Let us go to Bethlehem and see this event
which the Lord has made known to us."

It seems there were many who traveled the roads to Bethlehem all those years ago – Mary and Joseph, the multitude of people who filled inns and streets, the shepherds, the magi and Herod's soldiers. Bare feet and donkey's hoofs must have beaten the pathway smooth. A star, so we've been told, even pointed the way.

Why is it so difficult for us to find our way to Bethlehem today? Why have we allowed the pathway to grow over, the way to become unclear? Our paths to Bethlehem are filled with things other than dusty feet and starry nights. For many of us, during the weeks of Advent and even Christmas, our eyes are focused on shopping and baking, decorating and entertaining rather than on the Holy Child born in a manger.

While finding our way through the Christmas frenzy can be difficult, it is not impossible. By setting aside time to reflect on Jesus' birth and to worship together, we can experience a Christmas that is full of joy and promise.

First Week of Advent:
Longing for Safety and Security

Readings

The days are surely coming, says the Lord, when I will fulfill the promise I made to the house of Israel and the house of Judah. In those days and at that time I will cause a righteous Branch to spring up for David, who shall execute justice and righteousness in the land. In those days Judah will be saved and Jerusalem will live in safety. And this is the name by which the city will be called: "The Lord is our righteousness."

Jeremiah 33:14-16

(An Inclusive Language Lectionary, Year C)

For what thanksgiving can we render to God for you, for all the joy which we feel for your sake before our God, praying earnestly night and day that we may see you face to face and supply what is lacking in your faith?

Now may God, even God's self, and our Lord Jesus, direct our way to you; and may the Lord make you increase and abound in love to one another and to all people, as we do to you, in order to establish your hearts unblamable in holiness before God, at the coming of our Lord Jesus with all the saints.

1 Thessalonians 3:9-13 (paraphrase)

"There will be signs in the sun, the moon, and the stars, and on the earth distress among nations confused by the roaring of the sea and the waves. People will faint from fear and foreboding of what is coming upon the world, for the powers

of the heavens will be shaken. Then they will see 'the Son of
Man coming in a cloud' with power and great glory. Now
when these things begin to take place, stand up and raise your
heads, because your redemption is drawing near."

Then he told them a parable: "Look at the fig tree and all
the trees; as soon as they sprout leaves you can see for yourselves and know that summer is already near. Truly I tell you,
this generation will not pass away until all things have taken
place. Heaven and earth will pass away, but my words will not
pass away. Be on guard so that your hearts are not weighed
down with dissipation and drunkenness and the worries of
this life, and that day catch you unexpectedly, like a trap. For
it will come upon all who live on the face of the whole earth.
Be alert at all times, praying that you may have the strength to
escape all these things that will take place, and to stand before
the Son of Man."

Luke 21:25-36 (NRSV)

Reflection

In Milwaukee, one of the top tourist attractions is a place to eat. To get to the restaurant you go into an alley. On an alley door is a sign: "International Exports." When you walk inside you see a little office with bookshelves. A person sitting at a desk asks, "May I help you?" If you respond correctly, you say, "Is this a safe house?" At this the person pushes a button. Immedi- ately a bookcase opens and you walk through a maze-way to the dining area.

"Is this a safe house?" is a ques- tion many find strange in Milwaukee. Yet it is not a strange matter to mil- lions of people in our world. More and more we hear of children who are abused in their homes, torn apart by divorce, damaged because of violence suffered within the walls of their homes. Millions of us are wondering if we have safe streets and safe neighborhoods, as well as secure jobs and employment. Others around the world are being driven from their homes by wars and threats of violence.

The question has significance for many of us as we celebrate this first week of Advent. The question, "Is this a safe house?" represents the need and the longing in so many of us. Do we live in safe houses? safe neighborhoods? a safe world? If we undertake even a cursory reading of our papers, it would seem we do not.

Next to survival itself, safety and security are the most primitive needs of all humans. So, in a place where we long for safety and security in our homes, our streets, our jobs and our world, we are filled with hope when we hear the Lord's promise to Jeremiah. That promise to Jeremiah resounds to our generation on this first week of Advent: "In those days Judah shall be safe and Jerusalem shall dwell secure; this is what they shall call her: 'The Lord our justice.'"

This justice spoken of to Jeremiah and to us represents the core of right relationships. Without right relationships there can be neither safety nor security. Without justice between husbands and wives, parents and children, we can have little safety or security in our homes. Without justice between the rich and the poor, between one race and another, we will continue to be afraid to walk our streets or drive in certain neighborhoods. Without justice and right relationships, people around the world will resort to arms, threatening safety and security. Without justice we will continue to have wars and to plan for wars. People's needs for safety and security must be met if we are to have healthy relationships in our homes and justice in our society.

Where can we begin to make a difference so that "Judah shall be safe and Jerusalem shall dwell secure"? Maybe it will be in working within our own homes to make them truly "safe houses." It might be in the way we prepare for Christmas, knowing that Jesus calls us to remember the hungry, the sick, the imprisoned. It might be by joining Amnesty International, donating money to a hunger organization, or by serving the poor and oppressed in our neighborhoods.

Yes, the days are coming when "Judah shall be safe and Jerusalem shall dwell secure." We can begin to experience these days as we make a fit dwelling place for our God this Advent.

Questions to Ponder

• How do you experience a lack of safety and security in your home? in your neighborhood? in the world?

• How do your actions and attitudes cause others to feel unsafe? How is God calling you to work toward justice in your relationships?

• How might you express God's justice in your Christmas preparations?

Service

FIRST READER

The days are coming when "Judah shall be safe and Jerusalem shall be secure." The days are coming when our homes shall be safe, our cities shall be at peace and our world shall be secure.

SECOND READER

As we prepare to create a dwelling place for our God this Advent, we are invited to think, to pray and to plan for changes in our own lives that will help to realize God's promise of shelter for all people.

THIRD READER

People's needs for safety and security must be met if we are to have healthy relationships in our homes and justice in our society. Let us take a few moments to reflect silently on our own needs for security. Why do we need a safe house? *(After a minute or two of silence, encourage those present to share their thoughts.)* What are some reasons other people might need a safe house? *(Encourage brief sharing.)*

Lighting the candle

READER

We light this candle as a sign of God's promise to us and to all people for safety and security. Let our thoughts, prayers and actions reflect hope in the fulfillment of God's promise as we prepare for Christmas. *(Light the first Advent candle.)*

PRAYER

God of strength and tenderness, beneath the shelter of your wings the night harbors no terrors, only peace-filled stars bearing promise. This Advent we praise you for providing sanctuary and for directing us toward the promise. In peace we rest in your presence; in strength we go forth to make peace in the world. Amen.

Activities

1. Begin to think about a personal goal you can set to make one or several identifiable changes in the way you live and relate to God, others and yourself. Consider keeping a journal to record your progress and your feelings about the change(s) you are making. Encourage young children to draw pictures to express their experiences and feelings about making changes.

2. Discuss or reflect on what it means to be "safe" and "secure." What does it take for you to feel safe and secure in any given situation? (You may be surprised to learn that what makes you feel safe may be very different from what makes others feel the same.)

3. Look up the word "justice" in a dictionary. Think of a time when you experienced or witnessed injustice. Discuss how that injustice affected the safety and security of those involved. What can you do personally this week to see that someone is treated fairly?

4. This week, pray for strength and courage to recognize and speak out against injustice. Write a letter about a societal injustice you would like to see corrected and mail it to one of your government representatives or a local political leader.

Second Week of Advent: Living a Prophetic Theology

Readings

See, I am sending my messenger to prepare the way before me, and the Lord whom you seek will suddenly come to the temple, the messenger of the covenant in whom you delight – that one is coming, says the Lord of hosts. But who can endure the day of that coming, and who can stand when the messenger appears?

For my messenger is like a refiner's fire and like launderers' bleach; who will sit as a refiner and purifier of silver, and will purify the tribe of Levi and refine them like gold and silver, until they present offerings to the Lord. Then the offering of Judah and Jerusalem will be pleasing to the Lord as in the days of old and as in former years.

Malachi 3:1-4 (AILL, Year C)

I thank my God every time I remember you, constantly praying with joy in every one of my prayers for all of you, because of your sharing in the gospel from the first day until now. I am confident of this, that the one who began a good work among you will bring it to completion by the day of Jesus Christ. It is right for me to think this way about all of you, because you hold me in your heart, for all of you share in God's grace with me, both in my imprisonment and in the defense and confirmation of the gospel. For God is my witness, how I long for all of you with the compassion of Christ Jesus. And this is my prayer, that your love may overflow more and more with knowledge and full insight to help you determine what is best, so that in the day of Christ you may be pure and blameless, having produced the harvest of righteousness that comes through Jesus Christ for the glory and praise of God.

Philippians 1:3-11 (NRSV)

In the fifteenth year of the reign of Tiberius Caesar, Pontius Pilate being governor of Judea, and Herod being tetrarch of Galilee, and his brother Philip tetrarch of the region of Ituraea and Trachonitis, and Lysanias tetrarch of Abilene, in the high-priesthood of Annas and Caiaphas, the word of God came to John, the son of Zechariah and Elizabeth, in the wilderness; and John went into all the region about the Jordan, preaching a baptism of repentance for the forgiveness of sins. As it is written in the book of the words of Isaiah the prophet,
"The voice of one crying in the wilderness:
Prepare the way of the Lord,
make the paths of the Lord straight.
Every valley shall be filled,
and every mountain and hill shall be brought low,
and the crooked shall be made straight,
and the rough ways shall be made smooth;
and all flesh shall see the salvation of God."

Luke 3:1-6 (AILL, Year C)

Reflection

Last week we learned that there will be neither safety nor security in Judah or Jerusalem – as well as our homes, our streets and our world – if we do not have justice. And we learned that this justice is found in right relationships with ourselves, each other and our God.

Today Paul prays that we will be "rich in the harvest of justice." What does this mean to us in the church today? Especially, what does this mean when we live in the church, in political and state realities that don't always reveal a great amount of justice?

About a decade ago, church people in South Africa wrote a document called "The Kairos Document." In it they said there were three theologies at work in considering church and state relations in that nation. The first is called "state theology." When this was used then in South Africa, certain church groups would try to use the scriptures to justify the status quo of apartheid. The second is called "church theology." Church theology would call for reconciliation or peace, but do nothing to address the underlying problems of injustice. Finally, the writers of the Kairos Document spoke of a "prophetic theology" which stressed the changing of relationships that must take place among persons and groups and among systems and structures for God's work to be accomplished. Thankfully, we've seen the dismantling of apartheid and the increasing of hope that, despite problems, rough ways will be smoothed in that divided nation.

As we celebrate this second week of Advent, we might ask how these theologies operate within our own culture. A state theology "sprinkles holy water" on our economic system. Commercialism, consumerism, materialism and militarism often go unchallenged by our pulpits and church people. Somehow to challenge these makes one "disloyal" or unpatriotic.

Church theology in our culture calls for people to be reconciled, yet ignores the underlying problems of injustice, including policies and practices of exclusion. Women are told they should be submissive to their husbands. People are told to support the work of the church; and moneys are used for more buildings rather than for helping people who are poor. "Reconciliation" occurs in our churches only so long as certain kinds of people go to their own [churches).

Today's readings are prophetic theology at its best. Malachi wonders who will be able to "endure the day" when God's messenger comes. Then

John's voice echoes the same refrain. Certainly John's words about valleys being filled, mountains being leveled, windings made straight, and rough ways smoothed showed that he wasn't preaching state theology or church theology. John preached prophetic theology and paid for it with his head.

Do our concerns represent state theology, church theology or the prophetic theology of Malachi and John the Baptizer? If we are to truly have a right disposition this Advent and if we are to prepare for the reordering of relationships that is demanded of us this Christmas, we must get our priorities right. Paul calls it valuing "the things that really matter." What really matters for us as we hear the scriptures today, as we sit in the pews, as we drive our cars, as we go to the malls, as we prepare for Christmas? What really matters to our families? What really matters to our churches, our communities and our world? What really matters to us as a people, as a people of the promise?

Perhaps we should all read again, and make our own, that beautiful prayer we've heard from Paul's Second Letter to the Corinthians:

And this is my prayer, that your love may overflow more and more with knowledge and full insight to help you determine what is best, so that in the day of Christ you may be pure and blameless, having produced the harvest of righteousness that comes through Jesus Christ for the glory and praise of God.

Questions to Ponder

1. How can you begin to challenge the messages of the consumer culture this Advent season? How can your church address the commercialization of Christmas?

2. What does "reconciliation" mean to you? Think of ways we may try to smooth things over without addressing the underlying problems. What can we do differently?

3. Take a few moments to consider your preparations for Christmas. What really matters to you this Advent?

Service

FIRST READER

This Advent season, we are called to receive messengers of change who offer judgment or refinement for the wilderness within our personal and collective lives. *[If possible, read poet/messenger Alice Walker's poem, "We Alone," from the book* Her Blue Body Everything We Know, *Harcourt Brace Jovanovich, 1991. Encourage silent reflection.)*

SECOND READER

As we prepare the way of the Lord this Advent, we are invited to think, to pray and to plan for changes in our own lives that will help to realize God's promise of justice for all people.

THIRD READER

Messengers who bring judgment are rarely welcomed. Refinement is not really a pleasant experience. Think of refinement of ore into iron; the ore has to be melted down in very hot fire. Or, think of judgment like a cold shower; there is a degree of shock, of discomfort, but judgment, like a cold shower, can wake you up and energize you. Spend a moment in silence thinking about someone who appears to you as a messenger of judgment or refinement. What is uncomfortable in the message? What is energizing? *(Spend a full five minutes in silence. Children who find it difficult to sit still should be encouraged to draw a picture of their messenger or message.)*

Lighting the candles

READER

We light the first candle as a sign of God's promise to us and to all people for safety and security. (Relight the first Advent candle.) We light this second candle as a sign of our calling to prepare the way of the Lord. (Light the second Advent candle.)

PRAYER

God of the wilderness, a long time ago in Jordan you sent a messenger to prepare human hearts for the coming of Christ. That message has brought great confidence and joy to many people. God of our wilderness, help us to prepare the way today for your coming with repentance and compassion. Teach us to live in expectation of your prophetic judgment, that we may abound in love and be found rich in the harvest of justice. In this time of preparation help us to learn to value the things that really matter. In the name of the coming Christ we pray, Amen.

Activities

1. Think or talk about what really matters in life to you. What really matters to your family and closest friends? Why? Do you live your life in such a way that others know what is important to you; or do your words and actions reflect a different set of values? In your journal, make a list of areas in your life where your beliefs and actions don't match. (Encourage young children to draw pictures that represent their beliefs and actions.) What changes are you called to make?

2. As individuals or as a household, use magazine and newspaper clippings to make a paper collage of the things that are really important to you. Display the completed poster in a well-traveled area in your home. Use it as a daily check to see if your words and actions reflect the values mirrored in the collage.

3. Contact a local, state/provincial or national organization whose work and values match your own. Ask what you can do throughout the year to assist them in their work.

Third Week of Advent: Making Rough Ways Smooth

Readings

Sing aloud, beloved Zion;
shout, O Israel!
Rejoice and exult with all your heart,
beloved Jerusalem!
The Lord has taken away the judgments against you,
and has cast out your enemies.
The Ruler of Israel, the Lord, is in your midst;
you shall fear evil no more.
On that day it shall be said to Jerusalem:
"Do not fear, O Zion;
let not your hands grow weak.
The Lord, your God, is in your midst,
a warrior who gives victory,
who will rejoice over you with gladness,
who will renew you in God's love,
and will exult over you with loud singing
as on a day of festival.
I will remove disaster from you,
so that you will not bear reproach for it.
At that time I will deal
with all your oppressors.
And I will save the one who is lame
and gather the one who is outcast,
and I will change their shame into praise
and renown in all the earth.

At that time I will bring you home,
at the time when I gather you together;
indeed, I will make you renowned and praised
among all the peoples of the earth,
when I restore your fortunes
before your eyes," says the Lord.

Zephaniah 3:14-20 (AILL, Year C)

Rejoice in the Lord always; again I will say, Rejoice. Let your gentleness be known to everyone. The Lord is near. Do not worry about anything, but in everything, by prayer and supplication with thanksgiving, let your requests be made known to God. And the peace of God, which surpasses all understanding, will guard your hearts and your minds in Christ Jesus.

Finally, beloved, whatever is true, whatever is honorable, whatever is just, whatever is pure, whatever is pleasing, whatever is commendable, if there is any excellence and if there is anything worthy of praise, think about these things. Keep on doing the things that you have learned and received and heard and seen in me, and the God of peace will be with you.

I rejoice in the Lord greatly that now at last you have revived your concern for me; indeed, you were concerned for me, but had no opportunity to show it. Not that I am referring to being in need; for I have learned to be content with whatever I have. I know what it is to have little, and I know what it is to have plenty. In any and all circumstances I have learned the secret of being well-fed and of going hungry, of having plenty and of being in need. I can do all things through Christ who strengthens me.

Philippians 4:4-13 (NRSV)

John said to the crowds that came out to be baptized by him, "You brood of vipers! Who warned you to flee from the wrath to come? Bear fruits worthy of repentance. Do not begin to say to yourselves, 'We have Abraham as our ancestor'; for I tell you, God is able from these stones to raise up children to Abraham. Even now the ax is lying at the root of the trees; every tree therefore that does not bear good fruit is cut down and thrown into the fire."

And the crowds asked him, "What then shall we do?" In reply he said to them, "Whoever has two coats must share with anyone who has none; and whoever has food must do likewise." Even tax collectors came to be baptized, and they asked him, "Teacher, what should we do?" He said to them, "Collect no more than the amount prescribed for you." Soldiers also asked him, "And we, what should we do?" He said to them, "Do not extort money from anyone by threats or false accusation, and be satisfied with your wages."

As the people were filled with expectation, and all were questioning in their hearts concerning John, whether he might be the Messiah, John answered all of them by saying, "I baptize you with water; but one who is more powerful than I is coming; I am not worthy to untie the thong of his sandals. He will baptize you with the Holy Spirit and fire. His winnowing fork is in his hand, to clear his threshing floor and to gather the wheat into his granary; but the chaff he will burn with unquenchable fire."

Luke 3:7-18 (NRSV)

Reflection

The overall theme that seems to be at the heart of the readings for Advent is the need for a change in our lives, our relationships and our world. Hearing this, many of us might be like the different kinds of people who came to John the Baptizer and asked: "What are we to do?"

The very fact that all sorts of people – the crowds, the tax collectors and the soldiers – asked the question is amazing in itself. Today's statistics tell us that over 80 percent of church-goers don't even remember what was said in the Sunday sermon. Here you have the people not only listening to John's message and remembering it, but being touched by it enough to ask what they needed to do to make the Word come alive in their lives! What are we to do?

The crowds may have represented the average person in first century Palestine. These are the people who, today, we'd say paid their taxes, went to church and obeyed the law. Yet, even to these, John called for a reordering of their lives toward those in need: "Whoever has two coats must share with anyone who has none; and whoever has food must do likewise." The message is clear: We must also reorder our lives. We must go beyond paying our taxes, obeying the law and going to church. We must go beyond buying gifts for "those who have everything," beyond eating elaborate holiday meals, beyond hanging tinsel and lights. Like the crowds in first century Palestine, we are called to reach out to those in need.

Luke next tells us that "tax collectors also came to be baptized" and asked John "what are we to do?" In those days, tax collectors represented the political system that oppressed the Jews, and they often found ways to benefit personally at the people's expense. John tells the tax collectors, "Collect no more than is appointed you." The message for the tax collectors and for us is clear – even when systems, structures and forces seem beyond our ability to change, we can't allow ourselves to be part of the processes that hurt other human beings.

Finally, the soldiers ask John, "What about us?" And John addresses three tendencies those with power often face: don't bully anyone, don't accuse falsely, and be content with your pay. John's words speak to all of us who have positions of power. The question the soldiers asked John can be the question doctors and lawyers ask, the question repair people and salespeople ask, the question those hiring day laborers and domestics ask: "What about us?"

In all cases the message is the same: If we are to truly welcome the messiah into our lives and relationships, we should change our ways. By trying to make rough ways smooth in our world, we will be doing what we can to make God's reign come on earth as it is in heaven. Then we, too, can rejoice as we listen to the words of Zephaniah:

The King of Israel, the Lord, is in your midst, you have no further misfortune to fear. On that day, it shall be said to Jerusalem: Fear not, O Zion, be not discouraged! The Lord, your God, is in your midst, a mighty savior who will rejoice over you with gladness, and renew you with love.

Questions to Ponder

1. How is God calling you to reorder your life this Advent? Is God calling you to rethink the ways you celebrate Christmas? How?

2. Who do you have power over? Are you ever tempted to misuse that power?

3. The author refers to making "God's reign come on earth as it is in heaven." What does God's reign look like to you? How can you begin to make rough ways smooth?

Service

FIRST READER

"Whoever has two coats must share with anyone who has none; and whoever has food must do likewise."

SECOND READER

As we contemplate what we are to do this Advent, we are invited to think, to pray and to plan for changes in our own lives that will help to realize God's promise of justice and love for all people. *(Brief period of silence.)*

Lighting the candles

READER

We light the first candle as a sign of God's promise to us and to all people for safety and security. We light the second candle as a sign of our calling to prepare the way of the Lord. We light this third candle as a reminder of our calling to make rough ways smooth in our world.

Prayer

ONE: We turn to you, O God, as we open our hearts in worship and trust. We offer our lives to your people for we know that in the midst of our living,

ALL: Each of us can do something.

ONE: Our hands can build, heal and give comfort.

ALL: Each of us can do something.

ONE: Our feet can walk with those who suffer and are oppressed.

ALL: Each of us can do something.

ONE: Our eyes can be open and our minds sharpened to detect injustice wherever it might be found.

ALL: Each of us can do something.

ONE: Our tongues can speak truth to the powerful and name the evils that we see and experience.

ALL: Each of us can do something.

ONE: Even as we acknowledge our participation in these problems, each of us has the power to choose doing something over doing nothing. We find power and hope in the coming of Christ to bring with God a new blessing of freedom on the earth. Amen.

Activities

1. Discuss with someone the changes you are attempting to make in your life and relationships this Advent. How does it feel to make changes? Exciting? Frightening? Why? Talk about how God calls us to make changes in our lives, not just during Advent but throughout the year.

2. With God's help, how have you begun to make "rough places smooth" this Advent? Have you hurt someone by your actions or words recently? Visit, phone or write that individual. Arrange a time when you can discuss honestly what each of you can do to make your relationship deeper and more meaningful. Write about or draw a picture of this experience in your journal.

3. If you could give one gift to the world so that it might be a better place for all people, what would that gift be? Encourage each member of your household or group to find an object that symbolizes his/her gift. Individuals should box and wrap the gifts they chose and should place the boxes near the manger scene or under the Christmas tree. Leave the gifts wrapped until Christmas Eve.

Fourth Week of Advent: God's Words Fulfilled

Readings

But you, O Bethlehem Ephrathah,
who are little to be among the clans of Judah,
from you shall come forth for me
one who is to be ruler in Israel,
whose origin is from old,
from ancient days.
Therefore God shall give them up until the time
when she who is in travail has brought forth;
then the rest of the ruler's kindred shall return
to the people of Israel.
And the ruler shall stand and feed the flock in the strength of
the Lord,

in the majesty of the name of the Lord, the ruler's God.
And they shall dwell secure, for now the ruler shall be great
to the ends of the earth.

Micah 5:2-4 (AILL, Year C)

Christ, having come into the world, said,
"Sacrifices and offerings you have not desired,
but a body you have prepared for me;
in burnt offerings and sin offerings you have taken no pleasure.
Then I said, 'I have come to do your will, O God,'
as it is written of me in the scroll of the book."
When Christ said above, "You have neither desired nor taken
pleasure in sacrifices and offerings and burnt offerings and sin
offerings" (these are offered according to the law), then
Christ added, "I have come to do your will." Christ abolishes
the first in order to establish the second. And by that will we
have been sanctified through the offering of the body of Jesus
Christ once and for all.

Hebrews 10:5-10 (AILL, Year C)

In those days Mary arose and went with haste into the hill
country, to a city of Judah, and she entered the house of
Zechariah and greeted Elizabeth. And when Elizabeth heard
the greeting of Mary, the baby leaped in her womb; and
Elizabeth was filled with the Holy Spirit and she exclaimed
with a loud cry, "Blessed are you among women, and blessed
is the fruit of your womb! And why is this granted me, that
the mother of my Lord should come to me? For when the
voice of your greeting came to my ears, the baby in my womb
leaped for joy. And blessed is she who believed that there
would be a fulfillment of what was spoken to her from God."

And Mary said,

> "My soul magnifies the Lord,
> and my spirit rejoices in God my Savior,
> who has regarded the low estate of God's servant.
> For henceforth all generations will call me blessed;
> for the one who is mighty has done great things for me,
> and holy is God's name.
> And God's mercy is on those who fear God
> from generation to generation.
>
> God has shown strength with God's arm,
> and has scattered the proud in the imagination of their hearts,
> God has put down the mighty from their thrones,
> and exalted those of low degree;
> God has filled the hungry with good things,
> and has sent the rich away empty.
> God has helped God's servant Israel,
> in remembrance of God's mercy,
> as God spoke to our ancestors,
> to Abraham and Sarah and to their posterity forever."

Luke 1:39-55 (AILL, Year C)

Reflection

The gospel writers tell of God breaking into human lives and history through the story of two women – one old woman giving birth after years of trying to conceive and a virgin being with child. "Blessed is she who trusted that the Lord's words to her would be fulfilled," Luke writes of Mary. Mary was a woman who was open to God's will for her. A few verses earlier, we hear Mary's response to the task God wanted to entrust to her: "Be it done to me according to thy word."

In Luke, we are reminded of the amazing things God wants to do in each of our lives if, like Mary, we trust that God's words to us will be fulfilled. How does God want to enter our world today through us? Where do we find the presence of God in our lives, like Mary found it in hers and trusted that the Lord's words to her would be fulfilled? What is written of us in the book?

We read in Micah: "Thus says the Lord: 'You, Bethlehem-Ephrathah, too small to be among the clans of Judah, from you shall come forth for me one who is to be ruler in Israel.'" The one who came forth from Mary's body would be the ruler of Israel and of the church. This same one must be the ruler of our lives and our actions. On this day, one week before we celebrate his birth, we can still ask how we are preparing to welcome Jesus, to do his will, to trust that his words to us are being fulfilled in our lives.

The place where Jesus was born, "Bethlehem," offers us a clue. In Hebrew, "Bethlehem" means "house of bread." As we look around us, we see so many people in our world starving, so many malnourished, so many hungry, not just in places in Africa, but in our country where one of every five children is hungry.

Mohandas K. Gandhi once said something like, "If Christ would ever come again, he would have to come as bread for there are so many who are hungry." Jesus said to us that, if we will welcome him, it will be when we find him in the breaking of bread as well as in the serving of bread to the hungry. Today everybody who is called a disciple is called to become that bread for the life of the world. Every family is called to become a Bethlehem, a house of bread, where the hungry can be fed in some way. How might new life, new bread come to our households, to our church, to our nation and to our world this Advent?

If we can know what is written of each of us in the book, if we can see how our lives must be at the service of those who are hungry and poor at Christmas and throughout the year, then we can make these scriptures fulfilled in our lives. It is then, like Mary, we will be able to find him within us and among us. And then we, too, might hear those reassuring words, "Blessed is she (or he) who trusted that the Lord's words to her (to him) would be fulfilled."

Questions to Ponder

1. When all around us seems amiss, how can you trust that God's words will be fulfilled? What role might you play in the fulfillment of God's promise?

2. Where do you find the presence of God in your life? The author writes that we find God in our service to those who are poor and hungry. Is this true in your life? What other ways do you experience God's presence?

3. Do you find God present as you prepare for Christmas? What role does God play in your Christmas celebrations?

Service

FIRST READER

"If Christ would ever come again, he would have to come as bread for there are so many who are hungry."

SECOND READER

As we prepare to bear God into the world this Advent, we are invited to think, to pray and to plan for changes in our own lives that will help to realize God's promise of justice, love and bread for all people.

THIRD READER

In this final week before we celebrate the birth of Jesus, let us consider the ways in which, like Mary, we can find Christ within us and among us. *(Pause)* How are we preparing to welcome Jesus? Let us reflect in silence. *(After a short time of silence, encourage the group to share their thoughts.)*

Lighting the candles

READER

We light the first candle as a sign of God's promise to us and to all people for safety and security. We light the second candle as a sign of our calling to prepare the way of the Lord. We light the third candle as a reminder of our calling to make rough ways smooth in our world. We light this fourth candle as a reminder to watch for the image of Christ in the poor among us. May their absence serve to remind us of the divisions this celebration seeks to heal; and may their presence help transform us to be one body in the one who is to be born.

Prayer

ONE: We await you, Christ Jesus. There is room in our homes and in our hearts. We welcome your judgment of our lives,

ANOTHER: That we may be freed to love you and one another.

ONE: We welcome to our home the faithful and the doubters, the seekers and those who have been found,

ANOTHER: That we may know you as friend and redeemer of all.

ONE: We welcome your suffering,

ANOTHER: That in sharing it, we shall also share your joy!

ONE: With stranger, with neighbor, with friend, with those who are poor and those who are outcast, we await you,

ANOTHER: For there is room in our homes and hearts. We welcome you. Come, Lord Jesus, come. Amen.

Activities

1. How do you place trust in others? Is it difficult for you to trust others? Why? Make a list of those you most trust. What is it about those individuals that allows you to trust them? Think about or talk about how you trust God. What situations have increased your trust in God? decreased your trust?

2. Take a trust walk with another person. If you are in a group, break into twos. Have one partner blindfold the other, spin her/him around, and lead a walk around the house or yard. After a designated time, have partners change places so that everyone has a chance to be blindfolded and led on a walk. After the trust walk, reflect in pairs and as a group on your experiences.

3. How can you bring "new bread" or "new life" to your neighborhood or school? As a household, bake a loaf of bread and/or prepare a meal to take to a local homeless shelter or soup kitchen. Ask in advance if you can help serve the meal. On returning home, reflect on the experience. What did you see? hear? feel? How was Christ present? Write your thoughts in your journal.

Christmas Eve:
All Who Heard It Were Amazed

Readings

Isaiah 9:2-7 (see page 153-154)

> For the grace of God has appeared, bringing salvation to all, training us to renounce impiety and worldly passions, and in the present age to live lives that are self-controlled, upright, and godly, while we wait for the blessed hope and the manifestation of the glory of our great God and Savior, Jesus Christ. He it is who gave himself for us that he might redeem us from all iniquity and purify for himself a people of his own who are zealous for good deeds.
>
> Titus 2:11-14 (NRSV)

Luke 2:1-20 (see page 154-155)

Reflection

Each one of us probably has a Christmas crèche or at least a Christmas card that depicts the nativity scene described in today's gospel. The scene – Mary and Joseph, the child Jesus, shepherds, and maybe some angels in the distance – is etched in many of our minds.

Let's take a minute to listen to the gospel again, as though we've never heard it before. Verse 15 says that "when the angels left them," the shepherds decided to go to Bethlehem "and see this thing that has taken place." Verse 16 says, "so they went with haste and found Mary and Joseph, and child lying in the manger."

Now listen carefully to the next two short verses. The passage says the shepherds saw Mary, Joseph and the child in the manger. Then it says: "When they saw this, they made known what had been told them about this child." This, presumably, would refer to the message the shepherds heard from the angels. But then it says immediately, "And *all who heard it* were amazed at what the shepherds told them." Who was this "all" who heard the story from the shepherds? Was it just Mary and Joseph and their newborn? Were there others there?

Could the message be for us as well? Perhaps we've stopped being amazed by the story because we've heard it so often. The image of the nativity takes on new meaning when we place ourselves in our Bethlehems, in our places where the marginalized and rejected ones are forced to dwell.

Last Christmas I stayed in Milwaukee where I live among the poor. I went to my community's meal program and was especially touched by seeing the little children in the line for food. I thought to myself, "No child should have to be in a line like that. But, then, *that* child should not have had to be in a manger like that either."

Can we hear the good news today like those who heard it in far-off fields? Can we see what they saw in that manger centuries ago? Maybe we can't hear what they heard, see what they saw, or be amazed anymore at the sounds and sights contained in today's reading of God's birthing among us. Maybe we are like the people in today's first reading, living in darkness because we have taken the light among us for granted.

Or maybe we've seen the light, heard the angels, and perhaps even, at one time or another, paid a visit to Mary, Joseph and their infant. Only, then we went back to our fields, back to our work, away from our source, failing to let our eyes and ears of faith remind us of the vision we've experienced.

We can be among "all who heard it" if we are open to being amazed. We can be amazed at God's infinite love for us; amazed at the way God works in the human condition; amazed at who God chooses to be revealed to in our world; amazed that God is with us.

As we celebrate Christmas today, let's listen more carefully to the angels who may appear in our midst unannounced. Let's watch for the shepherds who may visit us in the appearance of poor and marginalized people in our midst. Like Mary, let's take a little more time to treasure these words and ponder them in our hearts.

Questions to Ponder

1. Who are the shepherds and angels in your midst this Christmas? Someone in your family? A neighbor? What messages do they bring?

2. The author found meaning in attending his community's meal program at Christmas. How might you place yourself in your "Bethlehem" this Christmas? What might amaze you there?

3. Can you see past the sentimental Christmas card images of the nativity to experience the amazement of God being born to a poor family in a stable? Is this how you would expect to see God-with-us?

Service

(Begin by singing a favorite Christmas carol or song.)

FIRST READER

The shepherds went with haste and found Mary and Joseph with the baby who was lying in a manger. And they spoke of the angels and all they had been told. And all who heard it were amazed. And Mary reflected on all these things silently in her heart. *(Spend a few minutes in silent reflection.)*

SECOND READER

This baby, Jesus, was born for us. By the power of the Holy Spirit, Christ was made flesh. Christ was born that we may be freed from chains of all kinds, and that we may receive the power to bring God's freedom to all people. This baby, Jesus, is born for all.

THIRD READER/SINGER

"How silently, how silently, the wondrous gift is given! So God imparts to human hearts the blessings from in heaven."

Lighting the candles

(Light the candles, including the Christ candle, in silence.)

READER

Let us be amazed. Our God has been born among us! Freedom has taken on flesh, and in Spirit dwells with us.

Prayer

O wondrous and loving God, you have been born among us and have called us each by name. You have gone before us, preparing the way: "The freedom of God is at hand!" Increase our capacity for freedom and love. Deliver us from any hesitation in the pursuit of justice. Encourage us in prayer, especially for those who are poor; those in prison; those who suffer from war, violence or hatred; those who are lonely; those who are sick; those who are grieving. Make us one through the unity of your presence. Be with us always, be with us now, O God who has been born among us! Amen.

Activities

1. Take a walk in the woods, in a local park, by a lake, or some other favorite outdoor spot. Observe the things around you. Select an object (rock, moss, plant, tree bark, etc.) and examine its detail. Reflect on the process by which it was formed. Was it formed in days, months or many years? Now imagine the birthing of God in a stable. What was it like? Imagine the sights, sounds, smells. Pray that by God's grace you will find increased wonder and amazement.

2. Find a quiet place of solitude on Christmas Eve or Christmas Day and reflect on changes you are making. Can you see clear signs of those changes? Can others? Write your thoughts in your journal.

3. Exchange your "gifts to the world" which you wrapped two weeks ago. Unwrap the gifts and try to guess who chose the symbol and what it represents. Talk about actions you can take to give these gifts to the world. How can you make rough places smooth? Close with a prayer that all these gifts may be realized in the world.

First Week after Christmas: Searching for Jesus

Readings

Samuel was ministering before the Lord, a boy wearing a linen ephod. His mother used to make for him a little robe and take it to him each year, when she went up with her husband to offer the yearly sacrifice. Then Eli would bless Elkanah and his wife, and say, "May the Lord repay you with children by this woman for the gift that she made to the

Lord"; and then they would return to their home ... Now the
boy Samuel continued to grow both in stature and in favor
with the Lord and with the people.

1 Samuel 2:18-20, 26 (NRSV)

As God's chosen ones, holy and beloved, clothe yourselves
with compassion, kindness, humility, meekness, and patience.
Bear with one another and, if anyone has a complaint against
another, forgive each other; just as the Lord has forgiven you,
so you also must forgive. Above all, clothe yourselves with
love, which binds everything together in perfect harmony.
And let the peace of Christ rule in your hearts, to which
indeed you were called in the one body. And be thankful. Let
the word of Christ dwell in you richly; teach and admonish
one another in all wisdom; and with gratitude in your hearts
sing psalms, hymns, and spiritual songs to God. And whatever
you do, in word or deed, do everything in the name of the
Lord Jesus, giving thanks to God.

Colossians 3:12-17 (NRSV)

Now every year his parents went to Jerusalem for the festival
of the Passover. And when he was twelve years old, they went
up as usual for the festival. When the festival was ended and
they started to return, the boy Jesus stayed behind in Jerusalem, but his parents did not know it. Assuming that he was in
the group of travelers, they went a day's journey. Then they
started to look for him among their relatives and friends.
when they did not find him, they returned to Jerusalem to
search for him. After three days they found him in the
temple, sitting among the teachers, listening to them and
asking them questions. And all who heard him were amazed

at his understanding and his answers. When his parents saw him they were astonished; and his mother said to him, "Child, why have you treated us like this? Look, your father and I have been searching for you in great anxiety." He said to them, "Why were you searching for me? Did you not know that I must be in the house of God?" But they did not understand what he said to them. Then he went down with them and came to Nazareth, and was obedient to them. His mother treasured all these things in her heart.

And Jesus increased in wisdom and in years, and in divine and human favor.

Luke 2:41-52 (paraphrase)

Reflection

Recently there have been many newspaper articles describing the decline in participation in Catholic and Protestant churches in Europe. At the same time another phenomenon is occurring: As the traditional parishes and congregations are becoming more empty, the shrines and the places of pilgrimage are filling up with standing-room-only crowds. Just recently someone told me of being in a small town in France where people passed by the local Catholic church, walking a mile further to the Benedictine monastery, to join the monks in prayer. In another part of France, people from all over the world and from all denominations visit Taizé, an ecumenical gathering place that is centered around prayer, devotions and celebrations that speak to people's desires to experience God-in-their-midst.

In North America, we are reading about the baby-boomers who are returning to church. Interestingly, though, they are not necessarily returning to the church of their youth or that of their parents. They are searching for places where they can be fed, where their longing for something more might be nourished. This brings us to today's gospel.

Mary and Joseph had been taught a pattern about religious practice. They inherited and continued a pattern of religious practice that involved certain assumptions, expectations and behaviors that indicated where they would experience God.

Following this pattern and passing it on to their son, Mary and Joseph took Jesus and went up to Jerusalem for the festival of the Passover. Unbeknownst to them, Jesus stayed behind in Jerusalem after the party left for home. Assuming they would find Jesus with relatives, neighbors or friends among the group, Mary and Joseph went a whole day without being concerned. When Jesus could not be found where expected, they began to search for him elsewhere. Mary and Joseph found Jesus in the temple asking questions and listening.

What are our assumptions about where we are likely to find Jesus? Many times we get so used to our regular religious patterns – Sunday worship, monthly communion services, annual celebrations – that we, too, have to be jolted like Mary and Joseph. We realize that Jesus just might not be where we thought we could place him, or in the place where we tried to put him. We must begin our search for him all over.

Today's gospel leaves us with an important message: to be near Jesus, we must never stop searching for him. Notice how many times the phrase "looking for" or "searching for" Jesus is used in today's gospel. Even Jesus uses the phrase, "Why were you searching for me?" Why do we search for Jesus? Why do many people have trouble finding Jesus in the places where we might expect to find him, in our parishes and our congregations? Where can we find Jesus in our temples today? How can we, like Mary, find Jesus in our hearts?

Questions to Ponder

1. Jesus was not where Mary and Joseph first expected him to be. Where do you expect Jesus to be? Where else might you find Jesus?

2. Why do you think attendance is declining in some churches? How can people better recognize Jesus' presence in the church? How do you find Jesus in your regular religious patterns?

3. Did you assume Jesus would be present in your Christmas celebra- tions this year? Were you "jolted" this Christmas?

Service

Lighting the candles

FIRST READER

These candles are lit as a sign that God's promise is never lost, that Christ's presence is with us throughout the changing seasons, and that we must never stop searching for Jesus in our day to day lives. (Light the four Advent candles and the Christ candle.)

SECOND READER

Like Mary and Joseph we search for Jesus.

THIRD READER

We will look among our relatives, ask our friends and neighbors, retrace our journey and ask ourselves and all we meet, "Where is our God?" We will search the paths of our heritage and the familiar roads of religion; we will recite the old catechisms and prayers and ask, "Where is our God?"

FIRST READER

When we have trouble finding Jesus where we thought we could place him, we can open ourselves to finding him in unexpected places.

SECOND READER

We will question our usual practices, and challenge our assumptions. We will listen and testify to personal experience of the Holy in our midst. We will look for Christ among God's people, especially those who are poor and outcast, and we will look for God in our hearts.

THIRD READER

We will never stop searching for Jesus.

Prayer

O Holy God, forgive us for our desire to keep you in one place for one time, in a little box at the front of the church, or folded within the pages of the Bible. The celebration of Christmas proclaims your life among us, unpredictable, spontaneous, full of joy and spirit. Help us to find you, that we, too, may be unpredictable, spontaneous, full of joy and spirit. We pray in the name of our teacher, the Holy Child, Jesus, Amen.

Activities

1. Describe or write about a situation in which you were searching for something or somebody. How did it make you feel? Why were you searching for this thing or person? Did you find the person or object in the place where you expected s/he or it would be? If not, how did you overcome your assumptions about where the person or object would be and begin to search in unexpected places?

2. Where are you most likely to find Jesus? Draw a picture. Discuss how you can begin to find Jesus in both traditional and non-traditional places.

3. Discuss how our limited assumptions about where God is and isn't found narrows our image of God. Make a list in your journal of ways you can expand your image of God. Note ways you can find God's presence in expected places and situations.

Epiphany (January 6):
A Call to Conversion

Readings

Isaiah 60:1-6 (see page 162)

This is the reason that I Paul am a prisoner for Christ Jesus for the sake of you Gentiles – for surely you have already heard of the commission of God's grace that was given me for you, and how the mystery was made known to me by revelation, as I wrote above in a few words, a reading of which will enable you to perceive my understanding of the mystery of Christ. In former generations this mystery was not made known to humankind, as it has now been revealed to his holy apostles and prophets by this Spirit: that is, the Gentiles have become fellow heirs, members of the same body, and sharers in the promise in Christ Jesus through the gospel.

Of this gospel I have become a servant according to the gift of God's grace that was given me by the working of his power. Although I am the very least of all the saints, this grace was given to me to bring to the Gentiles the news of the boundless riches of Christ, and to make everyone see what is the plan of the mystery hidden for ages in God who created all things; so that through the church the wisdom of God in its rich variety might now be made known to the rulers and authorities in the heavenly places. This was in accordance with the eternal purpose that God has carried

out in Christ Jesus our Lord, in whom we have access to God
in boldness and confidence through faith.

Ephesians 3:1-12 (paraphrase)

Matthew 2:1-12 (see page 163)

Reflection

The heart of today's gospel reading deals with conversion. How can we respond to the realization that the reign of God has come to us in the form of Jesus Christ? There are two ways. We can be like Herod, remaining in our positions of privilege and denying the invitation to conversion the announcement of Jesus' birth-among-us brings. Or we can be wise, like the magi, and seek to find him.

If we look closely at today's scriptures, we can see that the magi followed a process of seeking, finding and giving. Conversion begins with seeking. The magi searched for something greater than themselves. Herod and his advisors searched for the newborn king so they could keep in control.

The next step in conversion, after seeking, is finding. While Herod and his advisors found the text about Bethlehem that said where the newborn king would be born, they never found him. The magi followed the star to the place where Jesus could be found.

Once the magi found Jesus, they *gave up* their gold, their frankincense, their myrrh. They reordered the very possessions that must have meant a lot to them. Why? Because what they found was better. The magi found in Jesus a power beyond their own position, their own possessions, their own prestige. They put all of these on the line when they bowed before this newborn child. It was a sign that they had come to believe him to be the one who would usher in the reign of God.

In light of our Christmas celebrations, with all the gifts and glimmer, let's examine what really rules over us: our gold, our frankincense and our myrrh or the reign of God. This Christmas season, do we bow before the newborn child or the things and positions we've acquired? How many of us are willing to open up our coffers like those first truly wise ones did?

As North American Christians we find it difficult to consider reordering our possessions in such a radical way. All during Advent we *searched* for the right gift and when we *found* it, we were willing to *give up* "X" amount of money to purchase the gift. Too often we follow the steps – seeking, finding, giving – and experience conversion to the consumer culture rather than the reign of God.

Matthew's story of the search for Jesus has a lesson for us today. On the one hand, we can be so caught up in material things, in our own power, and even in our religion that we miss Jesus altogether. On the other hand, we can make him so much the center of our experience that we are willing to reorder our dearest possessions in order to live in his presence.

It all depends on whether we will be wise in the ways of the Herods of this world or wise like the magi. Let's pray that we can find the one whom alone we will serve.

Questions to Ponder

1. How might you miss Jesus in your pursuit of other gods? in your pursuit of power and prestige? Do you more closely identify with the magi or with Herod?

2. What role does God play in conversion? What are you called to give up? What are you called to receive in faith?

3. The magi gave up costly possessions when they found Jesus. What role do possessions play in your life? What are the gold, the frankincense, the myrrh in your life?

Service

(Light the four Advent candles and the Christ candle at the beginning of the service.)

READER

Epiphany is a time of endings and beginnings. The traditional 12 days of Christmas are ended. The season of Epiphany is begun. When we welcome Jesus as the magi did, we experience endings and beginnings. When we seek Jesus, we end our emphasis on material things and our reliance on our own power. When we find Jesus, we begin to reorder the ideas and possessions we hold most dear so that we may live in the presence of Christ. As this season of reflection, worship and activities ends, let us consider how we can make Jesus the center of our experience. *(Pause for a moment of silent reflection.)*

Prayer

ONE: Jesus, Holy of Holies born in a stable,

ALL: May you find your spirit in us.

ONE: Jesus, who loves common people and those who are poor and outcast; Jesus, who feeds the masses with the bread of life come down from heaven; Jesus, weeping with those who weep and rejoicing with those who rejoice,

ALL: May you find your spirit in us.

ONE: Jesus, delighting in the lilies of the field, the birds of the air, and the companionship of people everywhere,

ALL: May you find your spirit in us.

ONE: Jesus, persecuted by priests, mocked by scholars and slain by politicians; Jesus, who used the weak to confound the strong,

ALL: May you find your spirit in us.

ONE: Jesus, loving the children, agonizing for the lost, calling us to forsake all that we have; Jesus, power revealed in those whom the world holds of no account,

ALL: May you find your spirit in us.

ONE: Jesus, who calls us to reorder our lives and possessions; Jesus, promising peace and joy that none can threaten,

ALL: May you find your spirit in us. Lord have mercy. Christ have mercy. Lord have mercy. *(Share a brief period of silence.)*

Activities

1. Name one of your dearest possessions. Why is this item so special to you? Under what circumstances, if any, would you part with this possession? Talk about the role of possessions and material goods in this Advent/Christmas/Epiphany season. Is the role a proper or unbalanced one? What is the role of possessions in your life? What can we learn from the magi about reordering our possessions?

2. Review the giving suggestions in "Guidelines for Alternative Giving" (page 27) and "Reclaiming Christmas" (page 31). Were you able to incorporate any of these ideas in your Christmas giving? Did God call you to think differently about giving and your possessions? Consider practicing at least one of the suggestions in your year-round giving.

3. How has God called you to make changes this season? Discuss ways God has enabled you in this journey. Covenant together to make these changes lasting ones and to find new areas for growth. Write your thoughts in your journal.

Advent/Christmas Calendar

Lectionary Cycle Year A (1998)

Waiting for the Light

When faced with hunger, poverty, economic crises, and consumer pressures, it is difficult to find the joy, peace and fulfillment promised by the birth of Christ. But John 1:5 reminds us, "The light shines in the darkness and the darkness does not overcome it."

Beginning with the first Sunday of Advent and ending with Epiphany, this calendar offers daily thoughts and suggestions as you seek to bring God's light to the darkness of the world. Either individually or with your family or group, set aside a specific time each day – first thing in the morning, before or after dinner, etc. – to do the activities and reflections in this calendar.

December

5 Consider the words of Booker T. Washington: "I shall allow no man to belittle my soul by making me hate him."

6 Today is St. Nicholas Day! Spend time talking to a child about St. Nicholas, the patron saint of children. Give five cents for every child in your extended family.

7 Change attitudes about gift-giving. Write a letter to family and friends sharing your feelings about Christmas giving. Suggest gifts you would like to receive (i.e., a donation to a soup kitchen; a gift of their time).

8 Children can have difficulty understanding how they can "make this a better world." Fill a box with written suggestions: "Read a story to your brother"; "Collect aluminum cans to recycle"; etc.

December

9 Remember a difficult change you made in your life. What was your process? Did you do it suddenly or gradually? Was your decision made with public help or in secret? Perhaps you want to share this memory.

10 Make a list of the disposable products you use: razors, plastic bottles, diapers and the like. Next to each item write an alternative product you can use which is more ecologically sound.

11 Will you put up your tree this weekend? Don't decorate it completely – add an ornament each day so it is only finished on Christmas Eve. Give ten cents for each day your tree is up before Christmas.

12 Many people are struggling during these difficult economic times. When bombarded by consumer pressures, people can feel guilty or depressed. Can Christmas be joyous without spending a lot of money?

December

13 Today is St. Lucia Day. In Sweden, the oldest daughter, wearing a crown of candles, serves her parents wheat cakes and coffee in bed. Serve someone a simple, candlelight breakfast today.

14 Many people in countries around the world don't have access to clean drinking water. Give ten cents for every glass of water or can of soda pop you drink today.

15 Choose one or two Christmas cards from those you have received. Talk about or think about the person who sent the card. How does this person bring joy to your life?

16 Think of those who serve you and become their servant. Take a box of cookies to your local volunteer fire department; give some to the people who collect your trash.

17 In 1492 there were at least 43 million more Native Americans in the Western Hemisphere than today. Visit a Native American reservation or read a book on this.

December

18 Current paper recycling efforts save over 200 million trees each year. Give ten cents for every Christmas card you sent or plan to send which was not printed on recycled paper.

19 Visit someone in a prison, hospital or nursing home. Visit your local AIDS clinic.

20 Don't think of time spent waiting at a red light or in a grocery store checkout line as wasted time. Spend those moments meditating on the joy of Christmas.

21 Find out where the poor in your area live. Visit the neighborhood. What stores and businesses are there? What is the housing like? How does this community compare with your own?

22 Are you traveling to see relatives this Christmas? Think of Joseph and Mary's journey to Bethlehem. Give ten cents every time you eat in a restaurant during your trip.

December

23 Remember a time when you were afraid. Have you ever been fearsome in a crowd or community of people unlike you (i.e. people of another race or class)? Why? Give five cents for every time you remember.

24 In a group of family or friends, sing your favorite Christmas carols. Read aloud the birth of Christ and name five things each for which you are grateful.

25 In the evening, turn off all the lights except those on your tree, or light some candles. See how the light shines in the darkness for you and for your neighbors.

26 Read Acts 6:8-8:2. Today, St. Stephen's Day or Boxing Day, many people give boxes filled with gifts to the poor. Collect good used clothing, toys and books for those in need.

December

27 Remember a difficult time in your life or a difficult task you had to perform. Tell someone how you overcame this difficulty and who helped you, if anyone. Draw a picture of this.

28 Read Matthew 2:13-18. Due to Herod's wrath, the Holy Family became refugees. Today, there are 12 million refugees in the world. Write down reasons why people become refugees (war, poverty, etc.). Give five cents for each.

29 Thirty per cent of non-institutionalized senior citizens skip some meals almost daily. Give five cents for every can of food in your pantry.

30 Select a friend or a person in your family and tell them in person, by letter, in song or by a picture how much you care for him/her.

31 Think of three ways you can bring peace in the coming year. Give 25 cents for each New Year's resolution you make.

January

1 On a piece of paper write down three regrets or anxieties from the last year. Tear the paper into small pieces and throw them in the air like confetti. Pray, thanking God for new beginnings.

2 Reflect on this saying of Dorothy Day: "The greatest challenge of the day is how to bring about a revolution of the heart, a revolution which has to start with each one of us."

January

3 Invite someone less fortunate than you into your home for an Epiphany feast on Wednesday or a day next weekend. Treat the person as an honored guest. Rather than talk, listen to her/him.

4 Draw and cut out several candles from paper. On each candle, write one way you can bring light to the world (i.e., "Greet someone I normally don't speak to"). When you become a light in that way, display the candle.

January

5 On this night, long ago, the magi were very close to the place where the star was leading them. How might you have felt as one of the magi nearing the city of Bethlehem – excited, weary, joyous?

6 On Epiphany, the magi brought gifts to baby Jesus. Like the magi, journey to the organization you chose to support and offer your donation. If the organization is far away, send a letter of encouragement with your gift.

Sr. Joan Chittister, O.S.B.

Reflections on the Gospel Texts

Lectionary Cycle A

Activities by Karen Greenwaldt

First Week of Advent: Staying Awake

Readings

It shall come to pass in the latter days
    that the mountain of the house of God
shall be established as the highest of the mountains,
    and shall be raised above the hills;
and all the nations shall flow to it,
    and many peoples shall come, and say,
"Come, let us go up to the mountain of God,
    to the house of the God of Jacob,
that we may be taught in the ways of God
    and may walk in God's paths."

For out of Zion shall go forth instruction,

    and the word of God from Jerusalem.

God shall judge between the nations,

    and shall decide for many people;

and they shall beat their swords into plowshares,

    and their spears into pruning hooks;

nation shall not lift up sword against nation,

    neither shall they learn war anymore.

O house of Jacob,

    come, let us walk

    in the light of God.

            Isaiah 2:1-5 (AILL, Year A)

But of that day and hour no one knows, not even the angels of heaven, nor God's Son, but God only. As were the days of Noah, so will be the coming of the Son. For as in those days before the flood they were eating and drinking, marrying and giving in marriage, until the day when Noah entered the ark, and they did not know until the flood came and swept them all away, so will be the coming of the Son. Then two men are in the field; one is taken and one is left. Two women are grinding at the mill; one is taken and one is left. Watch therefore, for you do not know on what day your Sovereign is coming. But know this, that if the householder had known in what part of the night the thief was coming, that householder would have watched and would not have let the house be broken into. Therefore you also must be ready; for the Son is coming at an hour you do not expect.

            Matthew 24:36-44 (paraphrase)

Reflection

"Let us plant dates even though those who plant them will never eat them," Ruben Alves writes in *Tomorrow's Child*. "We must live by the love of what we will never see." Advent is the time of the church year that calls us to live by the love of what we will never see. At the same time, it is precisely the same part of the civil year that calls us to want only what we can see. The tension between the two is the great Christian tension of our time. Having everything we can get now is the national anthem of this society, the goal of our educational programs, the measure of a person's success. Until, of course, Advent comes and turns time on its edge, tips life off its business base and points us toward the future rather than the present.

Advent opens this year with two scenes. One is from Isaiah about the future to come. The second, from Matthew, tells us that it is our business to prepare for that future, to be ready for it by keeping our hearts centered, our vision keen, our lives sure and our commitment clear.

Isaiah says that, in the end, what Advent is really about is the creation of a new world in which there will be only one center, one people, one Light and one reason to be. "The mountain of God's house shall be established as the highest mountain ... and all nations shall stream toward it ... O house of Jacob, come," Isaiah pleads. "Let us walk in the light of our God."

The prominent Christmas message, however, the one that glitters from billboards and oozes out of Christmas advertising and seduces all the lines of children that troop to Santa Claus, is hardly that I must keep my eye out for the coming of the Christ. No, the ads want me to keep my eye on me. I'm to spend the season deciding what things I'll give and hinting at what things I'd like to get. I'm to forget about what I need to be so that the Reign of God can come, world unity can be and the Light can shine for everyone.

The ads are wrong, Matthew says. We have to learn to keep alert. We have to learn not to get immersed in the kind of tinny dailiness that numbs our souls, deadens our spirits, deafens our ears to the word, and leads, as a result, away from the mountain.

Advent reminds us not to get distracted by these other things at any season, not to get misled by the glitter, not to go after the baubles and bangles, but to move toward the mountain always. "In the days before the flood," Matthew reminds us, "the people were eating and drinking, marrying and being married, right up to the day Noah entered the ark. They were totally unconcerned until the flood came ..." They got all wrapped up, in other words, in daily activities and missed the Spirit. Unlike the people in Noah's time, we must make our lives seeds of a higher hope.

The fact is that we don't know when God will come into our own lives. We must wait and watch and be open and make ready.

Indeed, the questions for Advent are: How is God trying to come into my life right now? What is making the road to the mountain obscure or difficult for me this Advent? What should I be doing differently?

Service

QUESTION: What are we doing?

RESPONSE: We are getting ready for Christmas. Advent is a time to get ready to celebrate the birth of Jesus Christ. It is a time to be wide awake, watching for the new things God is doing in the world. We have made this Advent wreath to remind us to stay alert. Today we light the first Advent candle. (Light the candle.)

Q: How can we get ready?

R: We can listen. (Read Isaiah 2:1-5 and Matthew 24:36-44)*

Q: What else can we do?

R: We can decide that we will not let the glitter and bustle of the season distract us from seeing how God wants to come into our lives. Let us pray: You are the God who calls us to stay awake lest we miss your coming. Give us discipline to watch, wait and prepare for your coming. Give us courage to risk ridicule because it is your coming for which we wait.

Additional readings: Isaiah 43:14-21; Psalm 95; Ephesians 5:1-20.

Activities

1. Look at the local news reports (newspaper or television) to see if you can discover where God is doing new things in the world.

2. Talk with family members or friends about what it means to be awake. How often are we awake without being "awake" to God's presence and activity? What do we need to do this Advent season to wake up to that reality?

3. Take time each day (10 minutes or so) to wait for the Lord. How do we prepare ourselves to wait? What do we do while we wait? Give some examples of ways to wait.

Second Week of Advent: Realizing What Matters

Readings

There shall come forth a shoot from the stump of Jesse,
and a branch shall grow out of its roots.
The Spirit of God shall rest upon this branch,
the spirit of wisdom and understanding,
the spirit of counsel and might,
the spirit of knowledge and the fear of God.
And the delight of the one who comes shall be
in the fear of God.
That one shall not judge by what the eyes see,
or decide by what the ears hear,
but shall judge the poor with righteousness
and decide with equity for the meek of the earth,

and with words of judgment shall smite the earth
and slay the wicked with sentences.
The coming one shall be girded with righteousness,
and girded also with faithfulness.
The wolf shall dwell with the lamb,
the leopard shall lie down with the kid,
the calf and the lion and the fatling together,
and a little child shall lead them.
The cow and the bear shall feed;
their young shall lie down together;
and the lion shall eat straw like the ox.
The suckling shall play over the hole of the asp,
and the weaned child shall put its hand on the adder's den.
They will not hurt or destroy
in all my holy mountain;
for the earth will be full of the knowledge of God
as the waters cover the sea.

On that day the root of Jesse shall stand as a sign to the nations that this is the one whom they shall seek, whose dwellings shall be glorious.

Isaiah 11:1-10 (AILL)

In those days John the Baptist appeared in the wilderness of Judea, proclaiming, "Repent, for the kingdom of heaven has come near." This is the one of whom the prophet Isaiah spoke when he said, "The voice of one crying out in the wilderness: 'Prepare the way of God, make God's paths straight.'"

Now John wore clothing of camel's hair with a leather belt around his waist, and his food was locusts and wild honey. Then the people of Jerusalem and all Judea were going out to him, and all the region along the Jordan, and they were baptized by him in the river Jordan, confessing their sins.

But when he saw many Pharisees and Sadducees coming for baptism, he said to them, "You brood of vipers! Who warned you to flee from the wrath to come? Bear fruit worthy of repentance. Do not presume to say to yourselves, 'We have Abraham as our ancestor'; for I tell you, God is able from these stones to raise up children to Abraham. Even now the ax is lying at the root of the trees; every tree therefore that does not bear good fruit is cut down and thrown into the fire.

"I baptize you with water for repentance, but one who is more powerful than I is coming after me; I am not worthy to carry his sandals. He will baptize you with the Holy Spirit and fire. His winnowing fork is in his hand, and he will clear his threshing floor and will gather his wheat into the granary; but the chaff he will burn with unquenchable fire."

Matthew 3:1-12 (NRSV)

Reflection

The Talmud says so poignantly: It is not your obligation to complete your work, but you are not at liberty to quit it.

This week's scripture readings say much the same: We must go on and go on and go on in our attempts to make the world new, to make the vision new, and to make ourselves new.

"A shoot shall sprout from the stump of Jesse," Isaiah shouts. When it seems hopeless, new life will come. When it seems that things can not get worse, when everything we have counted on, when everything our society ever told us mattered fails – money and success and connections and achievement – and have been proved to be nothing but emptiness, lies and idle hope, then we can do what must be done. Then we can live the just life, the kind life, the Christ life. Something will come out of nothing. What has died in us will bring new life.

Advent, in other words, is the time for realizing what matters. The word of Matthew is quite clear: we should not prepare for Christmas by running from sale to sale. Our task, like John's, is to bring new life around us by preparing our own worlds for Christ.

When I won't participate in slipshod production at work, that's preparing my world for the integrity of Christ. When I refuse to make money by designing or developing instruments of war and death, that's preparing my world for the compassion of Christ. When I take steps to see that the poor, the elderly, the homeless and the less advantaged are cared for not simply at Christmas, but throughout the rest of the year as well, that's preparing the world for the Kingdom of Christ. When, like John, I learn to bear the ridicule that comes with shouting the vision of Christ to a world that is more comfortable with its own, that's preparing the world for the birth of Christ in its midst.

Today's Advent readings are about the world that is to be and the world that is now. It is my obligation, like John's, to enable this world with its war, greed and self-centeredness to be more like the world to come with its peace, justice and Eternal Sabbath.

Today's scriptures are unforgiving. There's simply no getting around them. Preparation for the coming of Christ is not about conspicuous consumption, or loving those who love us, or filling our lives with more and more things. Christmas, Isaiah and Matthew tell us clearly, is about our obligation to see that lions lie down with lambs, to see that there is "no harm or ruin on God's holy mountain."

We must ask ourselves: What one specific thing have I done this year to bring peace into the world? What can I do now, in preparation for Christmas, to make the world more like the Reign of God?

Service

Q: What are we doing?

R: We are getting ready for Christmas. Advent is the time for realizing what really matters. What really matters is preparing the way for the coming of Christ into our world with its war, greed and self-centeredness. Today we relight the first Advent candle, and we light one candle more. (Light two candles.)

Q: How can we get ready?

R: We can listen. (Read Isaiah 11:1-10 and Matthew 3:1-12)*

Q: What else can we do?

R: We can prepare the way for the coming of Christ – not by conspicuous consumption, but by the hard work of doing justice and making peace. Let us pray: We wait for your coming, O Christ. Stay by us in this time of preparation, that we may be energized to work for the world that you bring.

Additional readings: Psalm 72; Exodus 32:1-24; James 5:1-6; Matthew 25:31-46

Activities

1. Talk about what really matters to you in your life. Does God matter the most? Your family and friends? Your position and status in life? Your possessions? Your money?

2. What really matters in your Christmas celebration? Consider whether you are helping God to prepare for the coming of Christ into the world this year. What might you do differently this year?

3. Get the whole household together – or friends and relatives with whom you usually exchange gifts – for a discussion of alternative giving. Discuss taking an amount equal to 25% of the total money spent on last year's gifts and spending it on a birthday present for Jesus. Make a covenant on what is decided. You may want to consider writing a letter to other family and friends inviting them to join you in this covenant.

Third Week of Advent:
Reaching Out

Readings

The wilderness and the dry land shall be glad,

the desert shall rejoice and blossom;

like the crocus it shall blossom abundantly,

and rejoice with joy and singing.

The glory of Lebanon shall be given to it,

the majesty of Carmel and Sharon.

They shall see the glory of the Lord,

the majesty of our God.

Strengthen the weak hands,

and make firm the feeble knees.

Say to those who are of a fearful heart,

"Be strong, fear not!

Behold, your God

will come with vengeance,

with the recompense of God.

Your God will come and save you."

Then shall blind eyes be opened

and deaf ears unstopped;

then shall those who are lame leap like a hart

and mute tongues sing for joy.

For waters shall break forth in the wilderness,

and streams in the desert ...

The ransomed of God shall return,

and come to Zion with singing;

everlasting joy shall be upon their heads;
joy and gladness shall encompass them,
and sorrow and sighing shall flee away.

Isaiah 35:1-6 and 10 (NRSV)

When John heard in prison what the Messiah was doing, he sent word by his disciples and said to him, "Are you the one who is to come, or are we to wait for another?" Jesus answered them, "Go and tell John what you hear and see: the blind receive their sight, the lame walk, the lepers are cleansed, the deaf hear, the dead are raised, and the poor have good news brought to them. And blessed is anyone who takes no offense at me." As they went away, Jesus began to speak to the crowds about John: "What did you go out into the wilderness to look at? A reed shaken by the wind? What then did you go out to see? Someone dressed in soft robes? Look, those who wear soft robes are in royal palaces. What then did you go out to see? A prophet? Yes, I tell you, and more than a prophet. This is the one about whom it is written,
    'See, I am sending my messenger ahead of you,
    who will prepare your way before you.'
Truly I tell you, among those born of women no one has arisen greater than John the Baptist; yet the least in the kingdom of heaven is greater than he."

Matthew 11:2-11 (NRSV)

Reflection

Christmas has become a candy cane and sugar plum holiday created on Madison Avenue to convince us that life is meant to be a fairyland, full to overflowing with the goods of the world. If that's the case, neither classic spiritual wisdom nor today's scriptures are any proof of it.

Ancient mystics told the story of a seeker who searched for years to know the secret of success in life. Finally, one night a Sage appeared to the Seeker in a dream. The Sage said, "The secret of success in life is only this: Stretch out your hand and reach what you can."

The Seeker said, "No, it can't be that simple. It must be something harder, something more satisfying to the human spirit."

The Sage softly replied, "Ah, you are right. It is something harder. It is this: you must stretch out your hand and reach what you cannot." That is the message of today's scriptures and the message of Christmas as well.

In today's scripture, Isaiah is reaching for the impossible: fertile deserts and watered clay, lighter loads for those heavy ladened by life, joy for the joyless, hope for the hopeless. What Jesus brings, too, is not cornucopias for those already filled. Jesus brings impossible joy to those whose lives are limited by burdens beyond their control: "cripples walk, lepers are cured, and the poor have good news preached to them."

When John asks, "Are you he who is to come or shall we wait for another?" Jesus does not answer – see the rich get richer and the selfish get more satisfied. No, Jesus answers – the sign of the coming of the Reign of God is that the empty are filled, the poor are enriched, the oppressed are relieved. Jesus says that the sign of the coming of Christ is not the coming of things for the affluent; it is the coming of justice for the forgotten.

Perhaps the best thing about this scripture, however, is that we are there also, in John. Like John, we live in a grubby world where we must pay the price for trying to prepare the way for the word of God. The government finds John a threat and the people find him a disturbing presence. But John keeps reaching for what he cannot grasp. He reaches for Jesus and for justice. John knows what Advent waiting is all about. Advent is about bringing hope to the hopeless. Advent is about learning to recognize what peace on earth and good will is. Advent is about realizing what is demanded of us as well.

Even more provocative, perhaps, is that Jesus looks across the crowd, beyond the present and down through time, at us, and says, "What did you go out to the desert to see ...?" What were you expecting, in other words, when you reached out to embrace the Christian life: Madison Avenue or a journey to justice, commercial comfort or Christian challenge, Thou and I in gossamer privacy or Christian discipleship in the world?

"Reach out and grasp what you cannot," the mystic said. Reach out and become a better self. Reach out and make life better for others. Reach out beyond fences and worlds and build a brighter world for everyone. Reach out and make Advent real. No one finds the Christ without searching, without being open to the unlikely, the unfamiliar and the strange. No one finds the Christ without leaving one set of circumstances for another.

All of that takes stretching ourselves beyond ourselves. Isaiah knew that. John knew that. Jesus knew that. Now it's up to us. Reach out so that Christmas can really come.

Service

Q: What are we doing?

R: We are getting ready for Christmas. Advent is the time to ask, "Who is this One coming?" and, "What signs mark his coming?" Advent is the time to reach beyond easy answers. Today we relight the first two Advent candles, and we light one candle more. (Light three candles.)

Q: What can we do?

R: We can listen. (Read Isaiah 35:1-6 and Matthew 11:2-11)°

Q: What else can we do?

R: We can see that the signs of the Messiah's coming are not full Christmas stockings, but hungry people being fed, the homeless being housed, and the oppressed relieved. Let us pray: O coming one, we are anxious about your coming because we are not yet ready. Transform our preoccupation with comfort into compassion for those who suffer, that Christmas may truly come.

°*Additional readings: Psalm 146, Isaiah 61, 2 Corinthians 8:1-15*

Activities

1. Using newspapers, magazines, or other news articles, collect examples of ways that persons in your community are feeding the hungry, housing the homeless, and caring for others. Sort through these examples. Take out the ones that appeal to you. Think of ways that you can support the work that is being done in these examples. Next, take out the ones which offend you. Why are you offended? Then, look at both stacks, the ones which are appealing and the ones which are offensive. How is God's activity found in each example?

2. Making Paper Cranes: In 1955 a thirteen year old Japanese girl died of "the atom bomb disease" – radiation-induced leukemia. She was one of the many people to suffer the after-effects of the bomb dropped on Hiroshima in 1945.

   During her illness, Sadako buoyed her spirits by folding paper cranes. In Japan, the old myths say that cranes live for a thousand years, and that the person who folds a thousand paper cranes will have a wish granted. With each paper crane, Sadako wished that she would recover from the fatal disease. She folded 644 cranes before she died.

   In honor of her memory, Sadako's classmates folded 356 more cranes so that she could be buried with a thousand paper cranes. Friends collected money from children all over Japan to erect a monument to Sadako in Hiroshima's Peace Park, The inscription reads:

   > This is our cry,
   >
   > This is our prayer,
   >
   > Peace in the world.

   Each year people place paper cranes at the base of the statue to recall the tragedy of war and to celebrate humanity's undying hope for peace. By folding paper cranes to use as Christmas decorations, we show our hope and willingness to labor for the desire of all children to live in a world without war. (Find the instructions for folding paper cranes on page 68.)

Fourth Week of Advent: Receiving God's Promises

Readings

Again the Lord spoke to Ahaz, saying, "Ask a sign of the Lord your God; let it be deep as Sheol or high as heaven." But Ahaz said, "I will not ask, and I will not put the Lord to the test." Then Isaiah said: "Hear then, O house of David! Is it too little for you to weary mortals, that you weary my God also? Therefore the Lord will give you a sign. Look, the young woman is with child and shall bear a son, whom she shall call Immanuel. When old enough to know how to refuse the evil and choose the good, the child shall eat curds and honey. Before the child knows how to refuse the evil and choose the good, the land whose two kings you dread will be deserted."

Isaiah 7:10-16 (AILL, Year A)

Now the birth of Jesus the Messiah took place in this way. When his mother Mary had been engaged to Joseph, but before they had lived together, she was found to be with child from the Holy Spirit. Her husband Joseph, being a righteous man and unwilling to expose her to public disgrace, planned to dismiss her quietly. But just when he had resolved to do this, an angel of the Lord appeared to him in a dream and said, "Joseph, son of David, do not be afraid to take Mary as your wife, for the child conceived in her is from the Holy Spirit. She will bear a son, and you are to name him Jesus, for he will save his people from their sins." All this took place to fulfill what had been spoken by the Lord through the prophet:

"Look, the virgin shall conceive and bear a son,

and they shall name him Emmanuel,"

which means, "God is with us." When Joseph awoke from sleep, he did as the angel of the Lord commanded him; he took her as his wife, but had no marital relations with her until she had borne a son; and he named him Jesus.

Matthew 1:18-25 (NRSV)

Reflection

In today's scripture stories of Ahaz, King of Israel, and Joseph, spouse of Mary, we are confronted with two kinds of people. We see one who recognizes that he is face to face with the Mystery of life and risks getting involved with it, and another who comes face to face with the Mystery of life and, finding it difficult as well as mysterious, refuses to trust it.

We are called to realize that there is a great deal of Ahaz and Joseph in each of us that Advent is designed to expose and to heal. In the first scripture story of the day, Ahaz and Judea are faced with mortal danger from invading nations. The only answer, Isaiah instructs King Ahaz, is to rest absolute trust in God. He cautions Ahaz not to resist or to depend on the things of this world, but to do what is right for the people. "Ask for a sign, any sign," Isaiah challenges Ahaz. Hoping to look pious, Ahaz ignores God's invitation to request the sign by which he could know that God's will had been fulfilled.

"I will not ask for a sign," Ahaz responds to God. "I will not tempt my God!" I will not trust, in other words. I'll do things my way and the way of the world and Ahaz does and fails and destroys the people with him.

Disgusted with Ahaz's pretense to piety, God defines the sign anyway: "The virgin shall be with child..." Then and there, we get a glimpse of the divine economy. Here, down is up; poor is rich and weak is strong. In the divine economy it is trust and truth, not force and frenzy that save us.

In the second story, on the other hand, Joseph is faced with an equally difficult social situation and an equally incredible authority. An angel in a dream tells him to trust that what looks to him like disaster is really of God. Joseph trusts in God and saves the people by saving the Christ.

Like Ahaz, we so often go through life trying to look pious. We act as if our influence, our connections and our own power were enough to save us from the questions, doubts, difficulties and desires that plague us. Like Joseph, we get confused trying to choose good from better, salvation from selfishness. Like them, we wonder if we, too, will ever be freed from life's perils or be loosed from life's burdens. We then begin to concentrate on what we can amass to assure our security and prestige until, finally, we buy into the culture of death that depends on "deterrence," and the climate of comfort that depends on things that surround us.

Unlike Ahaz and Joseph, who were confronted with the promise only once, we are fortunate enough to be reminded every year that the virgin was indeed with child. We're reminded again every year that this is where hope resides. It's in the promise that we find real security and the purpose of life.

Advent is the time to remember Ahaz and his desire to save himself. Advent is also the time to remember Joseph, the one equally troubled by thoughts of social devastation but who, unlike Ahaz, heard the word of God and believed and so saved the people, without power, without force, without things. Advent is the time to remember the promise in our own lives.

It is so difficult to believe in what other people do not see. The powerful of the country believe only in amassing more "defense" at the expense of life everywhere. The clever of the country believe only in the survival of the fittest. The wise of the earth believe only in the amassing of wealth for its own sake. How shall we trust that strength and salvation and riches are not in those things?

Ahaz is our temptation, but Joseph is our model. We need to trust in God, not trust in things. That's what Advent is all about.

Service

QUESTION: What are we doing?

RESPONSE: We are getting ready for Christmas. Advent is the time to remember God's promises. Advent reminds us that real security and the purpose of life are found in God's promises. Today we light the first three Advent candles, and we light one candle more. (Light four candles.)

Q: What can we do?

R: We can listen. (Read Isaiah 7:10-17 and Matthew 1:18-25)*

Q: What else can we do?

R: We can resist the temptation to live – and celebrate Christmas – as if our influence, our connections and our own possessions make God's promises unnecessary. Let us pray: O God of Ahaz, Mary, Joseph and us all, we thank you for your life-giving promises. Open us to trust your promises, even when they make us uneasy.

*Additional readings: Ezekiel 37:1-14; Psalm 24; Luke 2:39-56; Revelation 21:1-4

Activities

1. Look at the scripture passages for the week, as well as the additional passages suggested. What promises has God made to the world? Do any of these promises make you uncomfortable? Why? How can you receive these promises?

2. Close your eyes and think about yourself at various ages. What were God's promises to you at those ages? When were you most receptive to hearing God's promises? What do you hear God promising you today?

3. If you know a child well, talk with that child about the birth of Jesus. Talk about what that birth means to the child and to you. What do conversations like this one teach you about the promises of God?

Christmas Eve: Gaining Wisdom

Readings

The people who walked in darkness
have seen a great light;
those who lived in a land of deep darkness–
on them light has shined.
You have multiplied the nation,
you have increased its joy;
they rejoice before you
as with joy at the harvest,
as people exult when dividing plunder.
For the yoke of their burden,
and the bar across their shoulders,
the rod of their oppressor,
you have broken as on the day of Midian.
For all the boots of the trampling warriors
and all the garments rolled in blood
shall be burned as fuel for the fire.
For a child has been born for us,
a son given to us;
authority rests upon his shoulders;
and he is named
"Wonderful Counselor, Mighty God,
Everlasting Father, Prince of Peace."
Of the increase of that government and of peace
there will be no end,
upon the throne of David, and over David's kingdom,

to establish it, and to uphold it
with justice and with righteousness
from this time forth and forevermore.
The zeal of the God of hosts will do this.

Isaiah 9:2-7 (NRSV)

In those days a decree went out from Emperor Augustus that all the world should be registered. This was the first registration and was taken while Quirinius was governor of Syria. All went to their own towns to be registered. Joseph also went from the town of Nazareth in Galilee to Judea, to the city of David called Bethlehem, because he was descended from the house and family of David. He went to be registered with Mary, to whom he was engaged and who was expecting a child. While they were there, the time came for her to deliver her child. And she gave birth to her firstborn son and wrapped him in bands of cloth, and laid him in a manger, because there was no place for them in the inn.

In that region there were shepherds living in the fields, keeping watch over their flock by night. Then an angel of the Lord stood before them, and the glory of the Lord shone around them, and they were terrified. But the angel said to them, "Do not be afraid; for see – I am bringing you good news of great joy for all the people: to you is born this day in the city of David a Savior, who is the Messiah, the Lord. This will be a sign for you: you will find a child wrapped in bands of cloth and lying in a manger." And suddenly there was with the angel a multitude of the heavenly host, praising God and saying,

"Glory to God in the highest,
and on earth peace among those with whom God is pleased!"

When the angels had left them and gone into heaven, the shepherds said to one another, "Let us go now to Bethlehem and see this thing that has taken place, which the Lord has made known to us." So they went with haste and found Mary and Joseph, and the child lying in the manger. When they saw this, they made known what had been told them about this child; and all who heard it were amazed at what the shepherds told them. But Mary treasured all these words and pondered them in her heart. The shepherds returned, glorifying and praising God for all they had heard and seen, as it had been told them.

Luke 2:1-21 (NRSV)

Reflection

"The wise," an ancient proverb says, "are torches lighting the path of truth."

Christmas Eve is about wisdom and what it takes to recognize the truth.

The problem is that today's scripture reading is drawn in contrasts that shock. The promise, both readings say, has at last been fulfilled. Everything we've waited for is with us. The fullness of time has come in our time. Everything we could ever want we finally have. The people rejoice. The angels sing. The truth has come. Everything is perfect. Except ...

Except we find the promise among the poor. We get the message from the marginal. We are confronted with the power of the powerless. The people who are present, the heralds of this new age, are simply not our kind of folks.

There's no status here, no trappings, no minions of the state, no credentials, no reverends, no one to impress. Jesus was born, you see, independent of both the Temple and the palaces of Jerusalem.

Clearly, the wisdom to be had here is that God is among us where we would least like to think, perhaps, and Jesus does not bring what the world teaches us to want.

The wisdom here is in the shepherds who had the sense to change their lives, and "in haste," in order to respond to the vagaries of the world around them.

The wisdom here lies in recognizing the peace of God in the unpretentious. The real power is found in the presence that threatens least.

The wisdom here lies in witnessing to these things – to peace without violence, to openness to the moving spirit of God, to satisfaction without satiation, to the presence of God in the lowest, the least, the last around us.

But this makes for a great deal of Christmas discomfort, in a society that stands for comfort and total security and status, even in its holiest season.

We like "peace through strength," we say. Then we spend the money of the poor on the militaristic agendas of the mighty. We don't have enough money for day care or education or job retraining programs in this country, we insist. We don't have enough money to develop the earth, but we have enough money to arm the heavens. Our peace is clearly not in the crib – our peace is in the sword.

We look for Jesus in the clean and the comfortable, not in the down and out, not in the uncouth, not in shepherds, not in mangers. We expect a syrup and butter Jesus, not the one who cleansed the temple or called the Pharisees hypocrites or told Pilate he had no authority over him.

Well, the angels are singing for us this year. The little people are still rejoicing. The shepherds are still trying to get us to see. Indeed, the torches are still being lit.

The question is simply whether or not you and I, too, will have the wisdom to find Christ this Christmas. Will we change our lives as a result of the finding? Will we welcome into the human race all those we persistently see as lesser, and cry "Peace to God's people on earth"? Or will we settle for only a very, very cheap facsimile?

Service

QUESTION: What are we doing?

RESPONSE: We are getting ready for Christmas. The waiting is almost over. This is the night when the Messiah comes. For those wise enough to see it, Christmas Eve is the night of good news and great joy. Tonight we relight the four Advent candles, and we light one candle more: the Christ candle. (Light all of the candles.)

Q: What can we do?

R: We can listen. (Read Isaiah 9:2-7 and Luke 2:1-21)

Q: What else can we do?

R: We can pray for the wisdom to find Christ this Christmas. Then, like the shepherds we can "make haste" to see what God has done. And, like the angels we can sing praises to God. Let us pray: Holy God enthroned in splendor, give us wisdom to allow our lives to be interrupted by your coming. Permit us to be so dazzled by your glory that our lives will be forever changed.

Activities

1. Listen carefully for signs that Jesus is born tonight. What are those signs? Make a list and share it with another person.

2. Find your favorite Christmas hymn. Sing the hymn or read the words aloud. Pay attention to the messages in the words. How do those words reveal the birth of Christ? How do you feel as you hear those words?

3. Turn off your radio, television, or other video or musical equipment. Listen to the voice of quietness around you. In the silence you may discover the voice of God speaking to you about the birth of Christ. What is that voice telling you? How will you respond?

First Week after Christmas:
Beginning Again

Readings

I will recount the steadfast love of God,

the praises of the Sovereign,

according to all that God has granted us,

and the great goodness to the house of Israel

which God has granted them according to God's mercy,

according to the abundance of God's steadfast love.

For God said, Surely they are my people,

children who will not deal falsely;

and God became their Savior.

In all their affliction God was afflicted,

and the angel of God's presence saved them;

in love and in pity God redeemed them,

lifted them up and carried them all the days of old.

Isaiah 63:7-9 (AILL, Year A)

Now after they [the magi] had left, an angel of the Lord appeared to Joseph in a dream and said, "Get up, take the child and his mother, and flee to Egypt, and remain there until I tell you; for Herod is about to search for the child, to destroy him." Then Joseph got up, took the child and his mother by night, and went to Egypt, and remained there until the death of Herod. This was to fulfill what had been spoken through the Lord through the prophet, "Out of Egypt I have called my son."

... When Herod died, an angel of the Lord suddenly appeared in a dream to Joseph in Egypt and said, "Get up, take the child and his mother, and go to the land of Israel, for those who were seeking the child's life are dead." Then Joseph got up, took the child and his mother, and went to the land of Israel. But when he heard that Archelaus was ruling over Judea in place of his father Herod, he was afraid to go there. And after being warned in a dream, he went away to the district of Galilee. There he made his home in a town called Nazareth, so that what had been spoken through the prophets might be fulfilled, "He will be called a Nazorean."

Matthew 2:13-15, 19-23 (NRSV)

Reflection

In one of the early writings of the Desert Masters the following tribute was recorded: "Abba Poemen said about Abba Pior," the desert monastics wrote, "that every single day he made a fresh beginning."

The faith for fresh beginnings is clearly one of the lessons of the first Sunday after Christmas. In Isaiah, it is God who makes the new beginning with a people for whom, it was now obvious, failure was to be a commonplace. By beginning again with a faithless people, God enables them to begin again as well.

In Matthew, Joseph shows us all how to begin again by carrying the Word himself. It is Joseph who shows all of us how to make life new by himself beginning over and over again. Joseph is sent first to Bethlehem, then to Egypt, then back to Judea and then finally to Nazareth. He went to all those places with steadfast love on behalf of the Word.

Today's scripture, clearly, is about the demand for steadfast love once the tinsel is down and the tree lights go out. However, today's scripture shows us the eternal beauty of that love as well.

God's steadfast love will sustain us this year, through financial struggles, family pain, personal confusion and national failures. It is God's steadfast love, the scripture assures us, that we can depend on, for "in all their affliction God was afflicted, and the angel of God's presence saved them."

It must be our steadfast love that enables us to begin again and again. Like Joseph, we must go to the Bethlehems of our own lives, to those places where those in our own family reject us, ignore us, irritate us, or need us. We must begin again to be kind and understanding and supportive of one another.

We must go wherever we are needed, not simply to the neighbors who are near to us, known to us and like us.

Like Joseph in Egypt, we have to begin again to carry the Word by showing steadfast love to the foreigners in our own lives. We need to reach out to the people whose skin colors are different, those who speak with an accent, those who have different values and those who believe in a world of a different shape.

We have to do more this year than simply speak to the foreigners in our lives. We must begin to go to them. We must learn to live well with people very much unlike us in background, culture and religion. We have to stop expecting the whole world to look and think like us. We must learn to love everyone steadfastly, despite differences, despite distances.

We have to begin again, like Joseph in Judea, to deal with those who are hostile in our lives without responding with hostility ourselves. We must begin to see that our task is not to destroy the enemy or to become emotionally and spiritually captive to the enemy that we carry within us. Our task is to learn to live well despite the enemy. We must see that the enemy does not become our excuse to be less than we can be.

Finally, like Joseph, we have to find the Nazareth that nourishes our lives, feeds our souls and directs our energies to the carrying of the Word with steadfast love. Every day we must make a new beginning to build the world of peace and justice in our own lives that Bethlehem promised, Egypt saved, and Nazareth nourished. We must begin and begin and begin with steadfast love.

Service

Q: What are we doing?

R: We continue to celebrate Christmas. The Messiah has come. A new year approaches. Life has new possibilities, and faith teaches new duties. Today we relight the four Advent Candles and the Christ candle to remind us that Christ's coming makes possible new beginnings. (Light all of the candles.)

Q: What can we do?

R: We can listen. (Read Isaiah 63:7-9 and Matthew 2:13-15)*

Q: What else can we do?

R: We can decide to make new beginnings every day and to resist the comfort of the status quo. We can reach out in compassion to those who – like the holy family in Egypt – are refugees in our midst. Let us pray: O God whose anger and despair at unfaithfulness are tempered by steadfast love, let our rising each morning be to fresh beginnings in faithfulness. Free us from the shame of taking your love for granted.

*Additional readings: Psalm 111; Deuteronomy 24:17-22; Colossians 3:12-17

Activities

1. Christmas was a few days ago. Think about how your life has been different since that time. What have you done differently? What might you do in response to that birth in the next few days?

2. Encourage children to do the word puzzle on page 72.

3. Who are the refugees in your town or city? Your state/province? The nation? What is your role in caring for them? What is the role of your church? What will you do?

Epiphany:
Following the Star

Readings

Arise, shine; for your light has come,

and the glory of God has risen upon you.

For shadows shall cover the earth,

and thick shadow the nations;

but God will arise upon you,

and the glory of God will be seen upon you,

And nations shall come to your light,

and rulers to the brightness of your rising.

Lift up your eyes round about, and see;

they all gather together, they come to you;

your sons shall come from afar,

and your daughters shall be carried in the arms.

Then you shall see and be radiant,

your heart shall thrill and rejoice;

because the abundance of the sea shall be turned to you,

the wealth of the nations shall come to you.

A multitude of camels shall cover you,

the young camels of Midian and Ephah;

all those from Sheba shall come.

They shall bring gold and frankincense,

and shall proclaim the praise of God.

Isaiah 60:1-6 (AILL, Year A)

In the time of King Herod, after Jesus was born in Bethlehem of Judea, wise men from the East came to Jerusalem, asking, "Where is the child who has been born king of the Jews? For we observed his star at its rising, and have come to pay him homage." When King Herod heard this, he was frightened, and all Jerusalem with him; and calling together all the chief priests and scribes of the people, he inquired of them where the Messiah was to be born. They told him, "In Bethlehem of Judea; for so it has been written by the prophet:

'And you, Bethlehem, in the land of Judah,

are by no means least among the rulers of Judah;

for from you shall come a ruler

who is to shepherd my people Israel.'"

Then Herod secretly called for the wise men and learned from them the exact time when the star had appeared. Then he sent them to Bethlehem, saying, "Go and search diligently for the child; and when you have found him, bring me word so that I may also go and pay him homage." When they had heard the king, they set out; and there, ahead of them, went the star that they had seen at its rising, until it stopped over the place where the child was. When they saw that the star had stopped, they were overwhelmed with joy. On entering the house, they saw the child with Mary his mother; and they knelt down and paid him homage. Then, opening their treasure chests, they offered him gifts of gold, frankincense, and myrrh. And having been warned in a dream not to return to Herod, they left for their own country by another road.

Matthew 2:1-12 (NRSV)

Reflection

Philip Sydney wrote in the 16th century:

> Who shoot at stars,
> though they never hit the mark,
> may yet be sure
> they shall shoot higher
> than those who aim at bushes.

And Emerson wrote, "Beware what you set your heart upon for it surely shall be yours."

The question is not how many magi arrived in Bethlehem. The real question we should ask is: How many of them started the journey in the first place? How many began but failed to persevere? How many saw a star but got discouraged at the length of the journey, the heat of the day, and the dull and dreary conditions of the trek? How many set their hearts on other things and settled down to live life on a lesser plane?

The real Epiphany questions for us are: What stars are we following? What stars are we failing to see and follow?

Isaiah says, realize what you have. Be everything you can be and you will become what you are called to be – a light to others. However, we forget that Christmas is as much a pledge as it is a boon. We've come to see Christmas more as what we get than what we are now obliged to give – ourselves.

There is so much of Christmas that is privatized now: my wish list, our family dinner, my church, our house decorations, our presents. Only the Epiphany can be counted on, if we get lost in all of that, to pull us out of ourselves again.

"Lift your eyes round about, and see," Isaiah insists, "They all gather together; they come to you." Indeed, see those who are following the star today. See the undernourished, undereducated, underdeveloped children of the Third World who are being sacrificed to pay back overbearing debts to First World nations.

See the staggering military costs of our own nation that will come back to haunt us in the schools not built and the arts not developed and the homes not constructed in our own country. See the people on the other side of town who work, but who are still poor. See those who are uneducated and so can't work. See the refugees on our borders who are looking for room in the wealthiest inn in the world and are being refused.

Like Herod, our world, too, says that it worships the child and is simply waiting to welcome him. Yet all the time the systems, the neighborhood and the country clubs fear what would really happen if the people did actually discover this star, this child, this God.

Perhaps the most telling part of the Matthew story is precisely this: that, having followed the star and found the Christ, the magi "departed to their own country by another way."

And there is a key: Like the magi, once we really see the Christ, we must begin to follow other ways. We can't go back by way of profit and power anymore. We can't proceed on the ways of division and oppression. We can't think like we used to: that salvation was mine and everyone else could take care of themselves. We can't want what we used to consider valuable anymore. Or, if we're not careful, we will indeed get what we set our hearts on and that would be a pity.

This Epiphany we are not called to follow a star. On the contrary, the purpose of Epiphany is to become a star.

Service

QUESTION: What are we doing?

RESPONSE: We are celebrating "Epiphany." The magi's long journey following the star ended when they offered gifts to the Christ child. At Epiphany we celebrate the "manifestation" of God's good news to all the world's people, those from both near and far. Today, for the last time this Christmas season, we relight the four Advent candles and the Christ candle. (Light all of the candles.)

Q: What can we do?

R: We can listen. (Read Isaiah 6:1-6 and Matthew 2:1-12)

Q: What else can we do?

R: We can give thanks for those who through the ages have followed the star to Bethlehem and so made that journey a possibility for us. In an age of cynicism, we can decide that we will not give up following the star. Let us pray: O God of

Bethlehem's star, let us not be among the Herods who seek the Child to thwart your will, but among the shepherds and magi who follow the star to offer obedience to the new King.

Activities

1. What gifts do you bring to the Christ child? Think of gifts that are appropriate. For help you may want to look back at some of the work you have done earlier during Advent and following Christmas.

2. Consider how Jesus is the light of the world. Think about where that light shines ... in the places of poverty and wealth, of brokenness and wholeness, of pain and health, and of light and dark. If children are present, help them to construct a star. Use any type of materials. As you make it, discuss ways that you can help to shine the light of the kingdom in those places.

3. Read again the passage from Matthew 2:1-12. Feel the joy that was present with the wise men as they followed the star to see Jesus. Talk about ways in which you can feel the same sense of joy as you approach the manger to see the newborn King. Discuss ways that you can continue to experience a sense of joy as the days move you away from the manger to the cross and the empty tomb of Easter.

Advent/Christmas Calendar

Lectionary Cycle Year B (1999)

Advent and Christmas Alternatives

Advent tends to be a time of doing, even stressful doing –
scurrying, shopping, worrying. Try some new doing this
season: waiting, preparing, anticipating, walking, receiving,
living, sharing. Each of these appears in this calendar. Watch
for them.

Go through the calendar with at least one "advent partner,"
face-to-face or by phone. A partner could be a friend or
someone you've wanted to get to know better. A partner is
good for support. And if a partner is a child, an adult can help
teach and serve as a role model.

November

28 Waiting in Hope. Pray, "God of Hope, open our hearts this week to all the ways you surprise us with Your presence. As we prepare for Messiah to dwell in our lives, strengthen us with patience. Amen."

29 Jesus' birth was a sign of hope for a people who were oppressed. The coming of Jesus continues to be a sign of hope for people who are poor and outcast. Who among us are in need of hope? Choose a cause or organization to support with money you collect while using this calendar. Decorate a can to hold the money. Give one dollar for each day you read the calendar without your advent partner.

30 Jesus' birth comes as a surprise – God's surprise, while people were waiting for the Messiah. Look for ways that God surprises you while you're waiting. Give 25 cents for each one you find today.

December

1 Be a surprise to someone else while you're waiting. Greet those around you while waiting in line at the grocery store. Share a beverage with someone while waiting for a train. Send a note or make a call of appreciation to a teacher, to a legislator, or to a business that promotes an appropriate understanding of Christmas. Sincerely compliment someone you've never complimented before.

2 We are a society that does not like to wait. Wanting quick results can cause stress. Counter that stress by doing projects, especially with children, that take time, such as planting seeds. Plant a Jesse tree (lilac bush) now and it will blossom by Christmas. Cover it with symbols from the Hebrew scriptures (star of David, dove, rainbow).

3 Christmas is a time of hope. Some hope for that special present. Others hope that everyone will just get along. Still others hope for time to relax. What are your hopes for this Advent season?

December

4 Waiting can be stressful, or a relief. Give ten cents for each potentially stressful wait that you turn into a relief – at a stoplight, picking up passengers ... Look for surprises while waiting: children playing, busy animals ...

5 Preparing in Confidence. Pray, "God, guide me to prepare myself and my world for the coming of Jesus. Give me the strength to make rough places smooth, to lift up those who are fallen. Amen."

6 Preparing for Christmas can be a time of great ups and downs. Make the rough times in your life smoother by maintaining a routine, by refusing to overextend yourself, by eliminating some seasonal stressors.

7 Think about who's carrying most of the load for your preparations. Reevaluate and talk about family and personal traditions and habits. Share the duties that you as a family decide to keep.

December

8 What word of comfort do you need to hear amid the December chaos? The Israelites were returning to a destroyed Jerusalem. God says to us, as to them, "I'm with you amid your disaster."

9 Write down all of the things you do to prepare for Christmas – making gift lists, baking, learning the music for the Christmas program at church. Give five cents for each item on your list. Are there other ways you can "prepare the way of the Lord"?

10 Take another look at the list you made Thursday. Are there items you could cross off the first list? What items left on the list could be simplified? Shared?

11 Isaiah is helping prepare the people to rebuild the temple in Jerusalem. What in our lives needs rebuilding, reorganizing? Relationships? Priorities? What old habits need changing? Choose one. How can changes happen gradually so that they "take"? We can emulate God's way of gentleness with ourselves and others.

December

12 Anticipating with Eagerness. Pray, "Creator God, we need help as we struggle to integrate our faith and our living. Let us look with joy to the coming year as a new chance to live as Your faithful child. Amen."

13 Read Luke 4:18-19. Write down some ways you can, like Jesus, reach out to the downtrodden and oppressed. Give ten cents for every idea on your list. Follow through on one of your ideas this week.

14 John the Baptist "walked his talk." He was a non-conformist, a "voice in the wilderness" – a lonely job. One of the tenets of voluntary simplicity is to "non-conform freely." In what ways can you "walk your talk" by non-conforming, especially in preparing for Christmas?

15 Rejoice in small events. Marvel at the crunch of snow. Behold light beautifully refracting through ice crystals. Don't make a list – just be open and aware of small pleasures.

December

16 Don't save celebrating just for "big" events – traditional holidays and rites of passage. Be open to celebrating *any* time. Ask, "What *else* can we do on Friday night?"

17 At supper, for a week, name three things that happened that day that made each person happy. Write them down. At the end of the week, read them all aloud. Donate 25 cents for each memory that still makes you happy.

18 It is just one week till Christmas. Set aside 15-30 minutes each day between now and December 25th to reflect on the meaning of the season.

19 Walking with Us in Love. Pray, "God of love, as You love us in forgiveness and newness each day, bless us to do the same. Open our eyes to see You in each person we look at this day. Help us make that part of our daily walk. In Jesus' name, Amen."

December

20 Sometimes we do things to try to vindicate our guilt. Singing carols at a nursing home, for example, may seem to help purge bad feelings about a shopping addiction. In what ways can we do good for the sake of others rather than to vindicate ourselves? Touch or hug the people at the nursing home. Commit yourself to coming back to see them again before next Christmas.

21 We want to control the way our gifts are used. How can we "turn it loose," anticipating that our gifts will be used worthily? How can we understand that all humans are imperfect and trust that God's love will prevail?

22 We tend to step out of our routines around Christmas and do special activities. Many touch our emotions, such as helping the Salvation Army or buying a gift for a needy child from an "Angel Tree." Anticipate with eagerness that these kindnesses will become part of our routine after Christmas. Commit to doing something every

December

month, such as supplying food to a community pantry, giving clothes or recycled school supplies to an agency, gleaning, distributing furniture to the needy, providing social awareness to students at a wealthy school.

23 We're on a journey with God. Greed is not a part of God's itinerary. In what ways does the commercialization of Christmas impose greed in our lives and tempt us to try to change God's itinerary? To get off God's path? To walk elsewhere, on a different path?

24 Christmas Eve – Receiving in Joy. "'Tis better to give than to receive" could also read "'Tis easier to give than to receive." Some adults have trouble receiving without returning the favor, without feeling indebted. Receiving humbles us. We may feel weak, even helpless. Jesus came for us freely. We respond by serving, not to repay but out of gratitude and thanks. How many ways can we receive with thanks?

25 Christmas. Some find it hard to receive a

December

compliment without a response of self-deprecation or a hollow compliment in return. Such responses label both the gift and the recipient unworthy. A simple "Thank You" is far better than "It was nothing."

26 Living with Grace. Pray, "Humble us to celebrate all that we have been given. Humble us for service to all who are in need. Humble us to give thanks for all that you have made us to be. In Jesus' name, Amen."

27 Unfortunately, when Christmas day has passed, many offer a sigh of relief, glad that next Christmas is so far away. Remember one joyful thing that was a part of your Christmas this year. Give thanks to God.

28 Part of the difficult job of receiving is expressing our needs so that they can be met. Expressing our needs opens us to being seen as needing help and also to the possibility of rejection. If you do not normally eat at a soup kitchen, eat a meal there, not as a server, but as a guest.

December

29 The Holy Innocents. From very early in its history, the church set aside this day to remember the massacre of children in Bethlehem by Herod's jealousy of the new born King of the Jews. Mary, Joseph and Jesus escaped to Egypt. Thousands of others did not. Think of the vulnerability of children today. Consider organizing a letter writing campaign on behalf of hungry children. Volunteer at a local shelter for abused women and children. Pray for children at risk.

30 Since Jesus has come, God accepts us. We can accept ourselves. Think about how you can celebrate how blessed and gifted you are. Make a Top 10 List of your talents. Be specific.

31 Make a New Year's resolution to let Jesus' love shine through you. Choose one way you can do this. Resolve to smile more, to spend an hour a week with a child or elderly person, to offer compliments and thanks more readily, to volunteer at a soup kitchen, etc.

January

1 God has made us special. God intends for us to use our talents for others. Choose one of your talents from your Top 10 List (from Dec. 30) and find a way to use it in a new way this year.

2 Sharing Our Treasures. Pray, "We are gifts of grace because You have called us Your own."

3 Like Isaiah, sing the praises of those who uphold righteousness. Sometimes we ridicule those who do what we know is right. Sing their praises until you're heard, refusing to demean those who do good. Direct, positive words are far more effective than a condescending or critical response. "I think she's a fine person" or "I thank God that he was in charge of that job" are simple and to the point.

January

4 Likewise, intercede when those who do good put themselves down or refuse your praise and thanks. Humility does not discount appropriate praise. A simple "Thank you" is far better than "It was nothing," "Praise God" better than "Don't mention it."

5 Knowing that God has forgiven us, we can forgive ourselves when we do stupid things. Give 10 cents for each thing you think of that you have not forgiven yourself for – big or small. Now pray for courage and insight to help you "let go" and forgive yourself.

6 The magi shared treasures with baby Jesus. How can we share our treasures – time, money, skills – with those around us? Give the money in your "giving can" to the organization you chose to support.

Tom Sine

Christmas Reflections

Lectionary Cycle B

First Week of Advent:
Waiting in Hope

Readings

O that you would rend the heavens and come down,

that the mountains might quake at your presence –

as when fire kindles brushwood

and the fire causes water to boil –

to make your name known to your adversaries,

and that the nations might tremble at your presence!

When you did terrible things which we looked not for,

you came down, the mountains quaked at your presence.

From of old no one has heard

or perceived by the ear,

no eye has seen a God besides you,

who works for those who wait for God.

You meet the one that joyfully works righteousness,

those that remember you in your ways.

Behold, you were angry, and we sinned;

in our sins we have been a long time, and shall we be saved?

We have all become like one who is unclean,
and all our righteous deeds are like a polluted garment.
We all fade like a leaf,
and our iniquities, like the wind, take us away.
There is no one that calls upon your name,
that bestirs oneself to take hold of you;
for you have hidden your face from us,
and have delivered us into the hand of our iniquities.
Yet, O Lord, you are our Maker;
we are the clay, and you are our potter;
we are all the work of your hand.

Isaiah 64:1-8 (paraphrase)

But of that day or that hour no one knows, not even the angels in heaven, nor God's Son, but only God. Take heed, watch; for you do not know when the time will come. It is like someone going on a journey, who, upon leaving home, puts the servants in charge, each with a particular task, and commands the doorkeeper to be on the watch. Watch therefore – for you do not know when the sovereign will come, in the evening or at midnight, or at cockcrow, or in the morning – lest the sovereign come suddenly and find you asleep. And what I say to you I say to all: Watch.

Mark 13:24-37 (AILL, Year B)

Reflection

Waiting ... we live in a world that knows much about waiting. Waiting for peace in Bosnia, Northern Ireland, and Jerusalem. Children in Haiti waiting hopefully for a chance to go to school. A young couple in Chicago waiting anxiously to secure a down-payment to buy a home. A pregnant teenager in Denver waiting expectantly for the birth of her first child.

The children of Israel knew a great deal about waiting, too. Isaiah pictures them waiting in eighth century BCE inside a fortified Jerusalem for the deliverance of God. And the liberator God did indeed deliver them from the siege of the brutal Assyrians. However, years later as a result of their unremitting disobedience, the children of Israel were taken into a galling captivity in Babylon, and again they found themselves praying and waiting for the liberation of God.

Isaiah 64:1-9 tells us something of a people who had learned to wait, but also something of the faithfulness of the God on whom they waited. "Since ancient times no one has heard, no ear

has perceived and no eye has seen any God besides who acts on behalf of those who wait for him." (Isaiah 64:4)

From "ancient times," the people of God have waited patiently for the coming of the Promised One of God ... confident they could trust the faithfulness of their God. In his novel *The Source*, James Michener pictures one small, devout rabbi who lived during the inter-testamental period, waiting expectantly for the promised messiah. Every Sabbath, the rabbi was the first to arrive at the synagogue for worship. He wanted to get the choice seat where he would be the first one to see the messiah coming down the road.

He approached every Sabbath with almost breathless anticipation. He waited all day long. And at the end of every Sabbath, he was always deeply disappointed. Yet, early on the next Sabbath, he could be found in his seat waiting again with expectant hope.

"In the fullness of time," the Promised One did indeed come As a result, our world, our institutions and the lives of millions of people have been forever changed by the coming of Jesus Christ. However, we still find ourselves waiting for the full advent of God in a world disordered and lives under stress, with this season commercialized beyond recognition.

When we fail to take time to wait in expectant hope, it is all too easy to be overwhelmed with all that is going wrong in our lives and our world. We often forget "the One who acts on behalf of those who wait for God." I am convinced that the greatest threat to our spiritual life is not sin but despair. I suspect that is why Dante wrote about the first gate into Hades, "Abandon all hope all who enter here." How can we wait with hope for the advent of Christ and share that hope with those who are in despair? Mark reminds us in this week's reading that we must wait with hope for the advent of Christ, and we must watch as well ... for signs of God's advent (Mark 13:24-37). What signs are there around us that show God's presence in the world?

Advent invitation

This season of joy can be a time of overwhelming demands and expectations. It is easy to forget the real meaning of the season. As we enter into a new season of Advent, I invite you to join others in a small Advent discipline of waiting and watching. Consider spending 15 to 30 minutes a day:

1. Waiting before God by meditating on the daily scripture for the renewal of hope;
2. Watching for and listing signs of hope in your life and in God's world that may be signs of the loving Advent of God;
3. Considering ways you can be a sign of hope for those in despair by working for greater justice for the poor.

Prayer

God of all Hope, as Advent begins, we renounce the despair that is all too ready to consume us. We covenant to wait for "the One who acts on behalf of those who wait for God" and to watch for signs of hope in our lives and in your world.

Second Week of Advent:
Preparing in Confidence

Readings

Comfort, comfort my people,

says your God.

Speak tenderly to Jerusalem,

and cry to it

that its warfare is ended,

that its iniquity is pardoned,

that it has received from God's hand

double for all its sins.

A voice cries:

"In the wilderness prepare the way of the Lord,

make straight in the desert a highway for our God.

Every valley shall be lifted up,

and every mountain and hill be made low;

the uneven ground shall become level,

and the rough places a plain.

And the glory of God shall be revealed,

and all flesh shall see it together,

for the mouth of God has spoken."

A voice says, "Cry!"

And I said, "What shall I cry?"

All flesh is grass,

and all its beauty is like the flower of the field.

The grass withers, the flower fades,

when the breath of God blows upon it;

surely the people is grass.

The grass withers, the flower fades;
but the word of our God will stand forever.
Get you up to a high mountain,
O Zion, herald of good tidings;
lift up your voice with strength,
O Jerusalem, herald of good tidings,
lift it up, fear not;
say to the cities of Judah,
"Behold your God!"
The Lord God comes with might,
and rules with a mighty arm;
God's reward is with God,
and God's recompense before God.
God will feed the flock like a shepherd,
gather the lambs in God's arms,
carry them in God's bosom,
and gently lead those that are with young.

Isaiah 40:1-11 (AILL, Year B)

The beginning of the good news of Jesus Christ,
the Son of God.
As it is written in the prophet Isaiah,
"See, I am sending my messenger ahead of you,
who will prepare your way;
the voice of one crying out in the wilderness:
'Prepare the way of the Lord,
make the paths of the Lord straight,'"
John the baptizer appeared in the wilderness, proclaiming a
baptism of repentance for the forgiveness of sins. And people
from the whole Judean countryside and all the people of
Jerusalem were going out to him, and were baptized by him in

the river Jordan, confessing their sins. Now John was clothed with camel's hair, with a leather belt around his waist, and he ate locusts and wild honey. He proclaimed, "The one who is more powerful than I is coming after me; I am not worthy to stoop down and untie the thong of his sandals. I have baptized you with water, but he will baptize you with the Holy Spirit."

Mark 1:1-8 (paraphrase)

Reflection

Preparing ... both Old and New Testament passages this Sunday urge us to "prepare the way of the Lord." As we prepare for the advent of God's new order, it is not enough that we wait in hope; we are called also to prepare in confidence.

Can we prepare the way of the Lord with confidence when many of us are struggling just to keep our lives together? Listen to God's welcome to the Israelites as their Babylonian captivity comes to an end: "Comfort, comfort my people, says your God, speak tenderly to Jerusalem and proclaim to her that her hard services have been completed, that her sins have been paid for, and that she has received from the Lord's hand double for all her sins" (Isaiah 40:1-2).

Amazingly, God actually invites this bedraggled, demoralized lot to join in preparing the way for the advent of God. Listen to the prophet's call to "prepare the way of the Lord; make straight in the wilderness a highway for our God. Every valley shall be raised up, and every mountain and hill made low ..." (Isaiah 40:3-4). Despite the often chaotic state of our lives, we, too, are invited to join with our God in preparing the way of the Lord. But what can we do?

A group of Christian leaders in a remote village in Haiti were desperate to see God's advent of justice break into a seemingly impossible situation. A brutal magistrate had killed one villager, wounded another, and terrorized the entire community.

When the situation became intolerable, the Christian leaders called for a day of fasting and prayer on a high mountain. The whole valley, except the magistrate and his wealthy father, gathered for passionate intercession to the God who promises to bring a new order into being.

Out of that day of prayer, three village leaders, at serious risk to their own lives, took their case to the government authorities. Incredibly, in just three weeks, the magistrate was fired, and the reign of terror was ended. The villagers were jubilant that their earnest prayers had been answered.

During this Advent season, how can we prepare for the way of the Lord in our communities? How can we seek to lift up those who are fallen or challenge the agendas of those in high places?

This is the season to allow our God to come to us in our personal lives, too, to lift us out of the deep valleys of fear, depression and anxiety. God also comes to pull down those high places in our lives ... our self-preoccupied agendas, our anger, our distorted sexuality, our resentments toward others ... to prepare the way of the Lord.

Advent invitation

During this second week of Advent, you are invited to join in preparing the way of the Lord. During your time of meditation each day, you are invited to:

1. List one way you can lift up those who are fallen or challenge those in high places ... and, prayerfully, follow through this week;
2. List areas in your own life in which you will both receive the encouragement of God, and you will, with God's help, remove those high places that set themselves against all that God intends for you.

Prayer

Preparer of the Way, we pray with confidence that this week you will enable us to join you in preparing the way of the Lord. Let us seek to bring down the high places and lift up the low valleys in both our lives and the larger society ... as a sign of the advent of God.

Third Week of Advent:
Anticipating with Eagerness

Readings

The Spirit of the Lord God is upon me,

because God has anointed me

to bring good tidings to those who are afflicted;

God has sent me to bind up the brokenhearted,

to proclaim liberty to the captives,

and the opening of the prison to those who are bound;

to proclaim the year of God's favor,

and the day of vengeance of our God;

to comfort all who mourn;

to grant to those who mourn in Zion –

to give them a garland instead of ashes,

the oil of gladness instead of mourning,

the mantle of praise instead of a faint spirit;

that they may be called oaks of righteousness,

the planting of God, that God may be glorified.

They shall build up the ancient ruins,

they shall raise up the former devastations;

they shall repair the ruined cities,

the devastations of many generations.

For I the Lord love justice,

I hate robbery and wrong;

I will faithfully give them their recompense,

and I will make an everlasting covenant with them.

Their descendants shall be known among the nations,

and their offspring in the midst of the peoples;
all who see them shall acknowledge them,
that they are a people whom God has blessed.
I will greatly rejoice in the Lord,
my soul shall exult in my God,
who has clothed me with the garments of salvation,
and covered me with the robe of righteousness,
as a bridegroom decks himself with a garland,
and as a bride adorns herself with her jewels.
For as the earth brings forth its shoots,
and as a garden causes what is sown in it to spring up,
so the Lord God will cause righteousness and praise
to spring forth before all the nations.

Isaiah 61:1-4, 8-11 (AILL, Year B)

There was a man sent from God, whose name was John. He came as a witness to testify to the light, so that all might believe through him. He himself was not the light, but he came to testify to the light.

This is the testimony given by John when the Jews sent priests and Levites from Jerusalem to ask him, "Who are you?" He confessed and did not deny it, but confessed, "I am not the Messiah." And they asked him, "What then? Are you Elijah?" He said, "I am not." "Are you the prophet?" He answered, "No." Then they said to him, "Who are you? Let us have an answer for those who sent us. What do you say about yourself?" He said,

"I am the voice of one crying out in the wilderness,
'Make straight the way of the Lord,'"
as the prophet Isaiah said.

Now they had been sent from the Pharisees. They asked

him, "Why then are you baptizing if you are neither the
Messiah, nor Elijah, nor the prophet?" John answered them,
"I baptize you with water. Among you stands one whom you
do not know, the one who is coming after me; I am not worthy
to untie the thong of his sandal." This took place in Bethany
across the Jordan where John was baptizing.

John 1:6-8, 19-28 (NRSV)

Reflection

Anticipation ... the children of Israel were uniquely a people of remembrance and anticipation. The Israelites were able to wait in hope, in part because they remembered the acts of God in their past. A major reason they were able to prepare the way of the Lord in confidence was that they looked forward to the promises of God for their future.

That's where many of us are in serious trouble. We often live our lives, struggle to raise our families and seek to order our private worlds with little compelling vision for tomorrow. We can become so focused on our own agendas, we have little time for those in need around us. We seem to have little image for the better future derived from our faith. Too often, we settle for giving our lives to the high stress aspirations and addictions of our upscale culture, attending church on Sundays ... if we have time.

John urges those seeking clarity and direction to consider Jesus "the true light" that gives light to every person who enters this world (John 1:9). To understand this "true light," we can seek to embrace the vision for the future that is at the very center of the life of Jesus and that first community.

To understand Jesus' vision for the human future, let's turn again to Isaiah's advent vision. In Isaiah 65:17-19, the prophet shows us a God intent on giving birth to a new heaven and a new earth. In Isaiah 2:1-4, the scene shifts to a new mountain and a new city. We see people coming from every tongue, tribe and nation to the great homecoming of God on the mountain of God. Then in Isaiah 25:6-9, we witness the enormous banquet of God that breaks out with jubilation celebrating a new age of justice and peace.

In this week's reading of Isaiah 61, we are compellingly shown God's purposes for the human future. We hear of a future in which the poor hear good news, the brokenhearted find healing, the captives are set free, and those who mourn are comforted; of a God who gives us beauty for ashes ... all because the Creator God "loves justice and hates iniquity."

Jesus made this advent vision his personal vocation. "The spirit of the Lord is upon me, because God has anointed me to preach good news to the poor. God has sent me to proclaim freedom for the prisoners and recovery of sight to the blind, to release the oppressed, to proclaim the year of the Lord's favor" (Luke 4:18-19, paraphrase). How are we called to follow Jesus in "proclaiming the year of the Lord's favor"? How can we transcend the commercialization of Christmas and the addictions of the American dream and put first things first?

Advent invitation

As this third week of Advent begins, are you looking for a renewed sense of purpose for your life and family? You may wish to join Jesus in making the advent vision of Isaiah your personal vocation by:

1. Writing a personal family mission statement drawing on the imagery of Isaiah 61;
2. Discussing how you and your loved ones might reorder your timestyles and lifestyles in light of your new personal mission statement.

Prayer

God of Loving Vision, enable us to follow the "true light" that has entered the world by making Jesus' vocation our vocation ... preaching "good news to the poor," proclaiming "freedom for the prisoners and recovery of sight to the blind."

Fourth Week of Advent: Walking With Us in Love

Readings

Now when the king was settled in his house, and the Lord had given him rest from all his enemies around him, the king said to the prophet Nathan, "See now, I am living in a house of cedar, but the ark of God stays in a tent." Nathan said to the king, "Go, do all that you have in mind; for the Lord is with you."

But that same night the word of the Lord came to Nathan: Go and tell my servant David: Thus says the Lord: Are you the one to build me a house to live in? I have not lived in a house since the day I brought up the people of Israel from Egypt to this day, but I have been moving about in a tent and a tabernacle. Wherever I have moved about among all the people of Israel, did I ever speak a word with any of the tribal leaders of Israel, whom I commanded to shepherd my people Israel, saying, "Why have you not build me a house of cedar?" Now therefore thus you shall say to my servant David: Thus says the Lord of hosts: I took you from the pasture, from following the sheep to be prince over my people Israel; and I have been with you wherever you went, and have cut off all your enemies from before you; and I will make for you a great name, like the name of the great ones of the earth. And I will appoint a place for my people Israel and will plant them, so that they may live in their own place, and be disturbed no more; and evildoers shall afflict them no more, as formerly, from the time that I appointed judges over my people Israel; and I will give you rest from all your enemies. Moreover the Lord declares to you that the Lord will make you a house ... Your house and your kingdom shall be made sure forever before me; your throne shall be established forever.

2 Samuel 7:1-11 and 16 (NRSV)

In the sixth month the angel Gabriel was sent by God to a town in Galilee called Nazareth, to a virgin engaged to a man whose name was Joseph, of the house of David. The virgin's name was Mary. And he came to her and said, "Greetings, favored one! The Lord is with you." But she was much perplexed by his words and pondered what sort of greeting this might be. The angel said to her, "Do not be afraid, Mary, for you have found favor with God. And now, you will conceive in your womb and bear a son, and you will name him Jesus. He will be great, and will be called the Son of the Most High, and the Lord God will give to him the throne of his ancestor David. He will reign over the house of Jacob forever, and of his kingdom there will be no end." Mary said to the angel, "How can this be, since I am a virgin?" The angel said to her, "The Holy Spirit will come upon you, and the power of the Most High will overshadow you; therefore the child to be born will be holy; he will be called Son of God. And now, your relative Elizabeth in her old age has also conceived a son; and this is the sixth month for her who was said to be barren. For nothing will be impossible with God." Then Mary said, "Here am I, the servant of the Lord; let it be with me according to your word." Then the angel departed from her.

Luke 1:26-38 (NRSV)

Reflections

Walking ... one of the absolutely astonishing claims of Christianity is that in the incarnation, God literally walks with us in Jesus Christ. It has been called the "scandal of particularity." During this fourth week of Advent, it is time for us to welcome again the coming of Emmanuel ... God with us.

We are reminded in 2 Samuel 7 that the God of the Israelites was neither a deity made of wood nor a God out of touch, but a deity who journeyed with the people of God. "Now therefore thus you shall say to my servant David: Thus says the Lord of hosts: I took you from the pasture, from following the sheep to be prince over my people Israel; and I have been with you wherever you went ..." (2 Samuel 7:8-9).

One cannot read the story of God in the Old Testament without being impressed with how intimately this Creator God journeyed with this difficult, stiff-necked people, sharing in the lives of their families, settling in a new land, and the all too frequent bouts of disobedience and rebellion. Here we find a God who not only travels with God's people, but a God who never gives up on them.

And this God was not content to simply journey with a small recalcitrant band. The Creator's love was destined to embrace a world. From the beginning, this God was intent on not only journeying with us, but entering, quite literally, into this creation ... through the life of one small infant.

The announcement comes for one frightened young Jewish woman in Nazareth. In the incarnation, the Creator not only enters into human flesh, but experiences the worst life has to offer, including humiliation, torture and death. As Jurgen Moltmann points out in *The Crucified God*, this is a God who knows first-hand and close up the horror experienced by victims of death squads in Guatemala, the sense of abandonment experienced by a young mother deserted by her husband in Los Angeles, and the health crisis facing a middle-aged couple in Milwaukee. This is a God who walks with us in all of our struggles and griefs. This is a God who, through Jesus Christ, fully enters into the worst the world can throw at us.

As we read further in the gospel, this Jesus, this "God with us," repeatedly invites us to walk with him ... whatever our circumstances. On this fourth Sunday of Advent, we can decide once again if we will accept this invitation and share with our companion God all the griefs and all the joys of our lives. And we can decide if we will embrace the disciplines that come with walking with Jesus.

Advent invitation

You are invited, with your family, a companion or on your own, to set aside an hour this week from the busy-ness and consumerism of the season to walk with Jesus. Read over today's gospel reading first, then go on a "prayer walk," seeking to enter into something of the jubilation, companionship and discipline of journeying with the God who asks to walk with us and who never gives up on us.

Advent prayer

God Emmanuel, we welcome with great thanks your visitation in Jesus Christ, and we gladly accept his invitation to walk with him and learn from him in the rigors of discipleship and the joy of friendship.

Christmas Eve: Receiving in Joy

Readings

Isaiah 9:2-7 (see page 153-154)
Luke 2:1-14 (see page 154-155)

Reflection

Receiving ... tonight we anticipate the ritual of receiving and giving. Flickering lights, the fragrance of pine boughs, packages spilling out in all directions. However, tonight's scripture invites us to come apart from the last minute busy-ness, wrapping of gifts and cooking of meals ... to receive from God.

Like those shepherds, we are invited to set aside the immediate that distracts us and fears that victimize us and hear again in wonder ..."to you is born this day in the city of David a Savior, who is the Messiah, the Lord." How like our God to come to us in a surprising way ... a baby in a cow stall.

But exactly what is this "good news of great joy"? First, we can recognize it as an immensely personal gift to everyone who will receive it. I have always been a Christmas person who delights in this season of family and festivity. However, it wasn't until I was 16 years old that I actually received the gift and entered into "the great joy."

During a church missions conference, I suddenly realized for the first time the very personal nature of the gift God was offering in Jesus Christ, an intimacy and reconciliation that I embraced eagerly with tears. Christmas has never been the same since. Now I not only share in the wonder of shepherds, but in the profound sense of all those who, throughout the ages, have chosen to follow Jesus and name him as Savior and Lord.

This Christmas Eve, we can enter into the great joy of this evening by rediscovering how deeply loved we are by the Creator God and how eagerly this God wants to give us the gift of intimacy, salvation and renewal for our lives and world.

It is essential, though, that we not forget this "great joy" is not for us alone, but for "all people." In Isaiah 9, we are shown a messianic vision of coronation and consummation. These recipients share a jubilation like that of an overwhelming harvest or the sharing of a treasure hoard. It is a future in which all the tools of torture, subjugation and oppression are destroyed and all military uniforms and equipment are burned in a huge conflagration at the coming of the Promised One.

The "zeal of the Lord Almighty" will indeed accomplish all of this. The Creator God wants to gift us both with a relationship to the divine and a world restored, all through the mystery of the birth of a child. We are invited the join the Prince of Peace in working for a future in which all oppression and violence is eclipsed by the shalom of God.

Advent invitation

On this Christmas Eve, you are invited to join with those you love to read these scriptures. Then, in an extended time of silence, receive afresh "the good news of great joy" both for yourself and for a world that aches to be made whole. Afterward, you may want to share with each other what you have received. Identify specific ways you can work for peace, justice and the care of creation, like supporting a church hunger program, the work of Habitat for Humanity, or Bread for the World.

Advent prayer

Author of Great Joy, we receive with deep gratitude the gift that comes to us and our world in the baby Jesus. We pray with all our hearts that your future will come and your will be done on earth as it is in heaven. May you make us agents of your justice and peace in anticipation of that day.

First Week after Christmas: Living with Grace

Readings

I will greatly rejoice in the Lord,
my soul shall exult in my God,
who has clothed me with the garments of salvation,
and covered me with the robe of righteousness,
as a bridgroom decks himself with a garland,
and as a bride adorns herself with her jewels.
For as the earth brings forth its shoots,
and as a garden causes what is sown in it to spring up,
so the Lord God will cause righteousness and praise
to spring forth before all the nations.
For Zion's sake I will not keep silent,
and for Jerusalem's sake I will not rest,
until its vindication goes forth as brightness,
and its salvation as a burning torch.
The nations shall see your vindication,
and all the rulers your glory;
and you shall be called by a new name
which the mouth of God will give.
You shall be a crown of beauty in the hand of the Lord,
and a royal diadem in the hand of your God.

Isaiah 61:10–62:3 (AILL, Year B)

When the time came for their purification according to the law of Moses, they brought him up to Jerusalem to present him to the Lord (as it is written in the law of the Lord, "Every firstborn male shall be designated as holy to the Lord"), and they offered a sacrifice according to what is stated in the law of the Lord, "a pair of turtledoves and two young pigeons."

Now there was a man in Jerusalem whose name was Simeon; this man was righteous and devout, looking forward to the consolation of Israel, and the Holy Spirit rested on him. It had been revealed to him by the Holy Spirit that he would not see death before he had seen the Lord's Messiah. Guided by the Spirit, Simeon came into the temple; and when the parents brought in the child Jesus, to do for him what was customary under the law, Simeon took him in his arms and praised God, saying,

"Master, now you are dismissing your servant in peace,
according to your word;
for my eyes have seen your salvation,
which you have prepared in the presence of all peoples,
a light for revelation to the Gentiles
and for glory to your people Israel."

And the child's father and mother were amazed at what was being said about him. Then Simeon blessed them and said to his mother Mary, "This child is destined for the falling and the rising of many in Israel, and to be a sign that will be opposed so that the inner thoughts of many will be revealed – and a sword will pierce your own soul too."

There was also a prophet, Anna the daughter of Phanuel, of the tribe of Asher. She was of a great age, having lived with her husband seven years after her marriage, then as a widow to the age of eighty-four. She never left the temple but worshiped there with fasting and prayer night and day. At that moment she came, and began to praise God and to speak about the child to all who were looking for the redemption of Jerusalem.

When they had finished everything required by the law of the Lord, they returned to Galilee, to their own town of Nazareth. The child grew and became strong, filled with wisdom; and the favor of God was upon him.

Luke 2:22-40 (NRSV)

Living ... of course the celebration doesn't end with Christmas. If we have received anything of the gifts of God, then we have the opportunity of living with the grace of God. In the gospel reading today, the infant Jesus has already become a young boy, and we are told that "the grace of God was upon him."

Once, my spiritual director asked me to spend a week meditating on the childhood of Jesus. At first, it seemed like an impossible task – there is so little narrative. What was immediately evident, though, is that the grace of God was on the life of this young child in a very distinctive way. In fact, it strongly reminded me of another young man, David. What they seemed to have shared was the way they both turned their lives toward their God with a singleness of heart that was unique.

Isaiah foresaw the coming of King David's heir. As you remember, Jesus chose the first portion of Isaiah 61 as his inaugural. In Isaiah 61:10-11, we are shown one who delights in the Lord because he has been clothed in the garments of salvation like a bridegroom and God makes the garden of the nations burst into praise before him. Finally, the prophet says of this one "you will be a crown of splendor in the Lord's hand and a royal diadem in the hand of your God" (Isaiah 62:3).

As followers of this Jesus and as sons and daughters of David, we, too, can know something of that special grace of God in our own lives. If any of us turn our lives toward God in even the slightest way, we immediately experience afresh the mercy of the God who delights in responsive children.

But if we turn our lives singularly toward the gracious Creator, we, too, can know something of that special grace that crowned the life of David and Jesus.

My friend Tom is a man touched by that "special grace." Like his master, he is a carpenter by trade. In his youth, out of his commitment to God, he took vows as a Trappist novitiate. After 11 years as a Trappist monk working in the wood shop at an abbey in Oregon, his health failed. Tom left the order and met Ida, and they shared a lovely family of four children. Despite hardships, Tom and his family have devoted themselves to working with people who are disabled through the L'Arche community, as well as working with people who are poor through their local parish. Recently, Tom lost Ida to cancer, and he is now raising his family alone. You don't have to be with Tom for very long before you discover in this quiet, unassuming man something of the special grace of God.

As a new year approaches, we all sense both new challenges and new opportunities. Chief among those opportunities is, like the boy Jesus, to turn our lives singularly toward the God who calls us. If we do, I am sure that, like my friend Tom, people will begin to recognize that special touch that graces our lives and bears witness to the God of all mercy.

Christmas invitation

Imagine what it would mean to "turn your life singularly toward God." As the new year approaches, consider setting aside time to take stock of your life, and to recommit your life afresh, with the single-mindedness of a young child, to the God of the epiphany, with the full assurance that not only the grace of God will go with us, but with the confidence that God will direct our path. Discuss with your companions how you might set aside a daily time to renew this commit ment and wait in silence for the God who calls us.

Christmas prayer

God of all grace, make us again like a young child who, with single-hearted devotion, turns to you. May we in this new year walk in your grace and be sustained by your mercy.

Epiphany (January 6): Sharing Our Treasures

Readings

Isaiah 60:1-6 (see page 162)

Matthew 2:1-12 (see page 163)

Reflection

Sharing ... at the very center of the Gospel of Jesus Christ is the gift of sharing. As Jesus was a man for others, we are called to be a people for others. In the two readings for today, we are shown images of people sharing their treasures out of devotion to God. In the passage of Isaiah 60:1-6, we see people from all nations converging on Jerusalem at the great homecoming of God, bringing their treasures with them.

Picture the brilliant imagery of the prophet as he describes the grand homecoming scene in Jerusalem: "Arise shine for your light has come and the glory of the Lord rises upon you ... lift up your eyes and look about you; all assembled come to you; your sons come from afar and your daughters are carried on arms ... the wealth of the nations will be brought to you, to you the riches of the nations will come ..." (Isaiah 60:1-5)

In the readings from Matthew 2:1-12, we are shown the wise men bringing their treasures to Jesus as an expression of their worship. We are still invited to bring our treasures to Jesus. There is no better time than at the beginning of a new year to reexamine how we use our resources and to discover how much we have to share.

It is clear from the gospels that those who chose to follow Jesus not only shared their treasures, they committed their entire lives both to God and the teachings of God that have filled these advent readings. What does Jesus ask of us?

Jesus' teachings tell of the inbreaking of God's new order of justice, peace and righteousness, and also call us to stewardship of our lives and resources. While Jewish teachings emphasized the tithe, a growing number of New Testament scholars tell us that the New Testament calls us to something more – to whole life stewardship.

Recently while traveling in Britain, I learned of a couple in Cambridge who found some creative ways to reduce their lifestyle costs so they could each cut their work schedule to 20 hours a week. Their reason? They wanted to invest the other 20 hours a week in working with Jesus' mission to those in need in their community.

As we stand at the threshold of the Third Millennium, human need is escalating throughout our world. At the same time, needs among people who are poor are increasing in North American society, we are seeing drastic cutbacks in social programs. Furthermore, the church in North America, like the church throughout the Western world, is slowly shrinking, and its capacity to respond to this growing need is also gradually declining.

Those of us who follow Jesus are called to seriously reexamine how we prioritize our use of time and resources in relationship to Christ's mission "to bring good news to the poor, recovery of sight to the blind and set at liberty those who are captive." I am convinced that if we each in our own ways choose to put God's purposes first, we will be surprised at how God will use our mustard seeds. I believe that through whole life stewardship, we can create a way of life that is both more festive and less stressed, a way of life in which we have more "treasures," like the wise men, to bring in devotion to Jesus.

Epiphany invitation

As we enter a new year, we are invited to reexamine prayerfully our timestyles and our lifestyles to discover how we can, like those first disciples, put God first in our lives and families. Consider drafting new stewardship goals for the new year. How might you reorder your private world to free up more time and money to invest in enabling people in need to help themselves?

Epiphany prayer

God of extravagant generosity, we come to you with few treasures to offer except our own lives. We willingly give them back to you. By your grace make us determined, like the Jesus we follow, to put first things first. Lead us as we more fully invest our lives in the advancing of your kingdom in response to the escalating challenges of a new millennium.

Additional services

These services are designed to be used with events, whenever they may occur, rather than on specific dates.

You are urged to select an appropriate reflection to accompany the service. If, for example, you use the Service for Planning Your Gift-Giving around the First Sunday in Advent, then use the reflection written for that day.

Service for Planning Gift-Giving

Ashley Nedeau-Owen

(A child begins the service by giving a Bible to any adult, without coaching. That adult becomes the leader.)

LEADER: Let us hold hands in a circle, bow our heads and pray. Thank you God for giving us a child to choose us to follow you. Bestow your wisdom upon us as we make difficult gift decisions this season. Help us to make our gift-giving reflect your presence in our lives and in the lives of those to whom we give. In Jesus' name, amen.

Gifts chosen wisely have real value. They cannot be given a dollar value nor can they keep up with current fashion. Let us share well chosen stories about meaningful gifts.

(Each person speaks in turn.) "The gift that I still treasure most is one I received from (name the giver). I treasure it because ..."

LEADER: The gift of "whole, healthy relationships" is a gift that God gave through Jesus. As we plan our gift-giving, let us focus on our relationships with family, friends and co-workers. Then focus on our home, our place of worship and our relationship with the whole earth ... the environment and the people. Let us examine our relationship to money and to business and advertising. Are each of these relationships healthy?

Gift-giving has impacts that we may never see. It may be simple or complex. Let's strive to make ours thoughtful, meaningful for the givers and the receivers.

(If appropriate, read the reflection for the day that this service is used.)

Service for Trimming the Christmas Tree

Rick Hoffarth

Our society is diverse. So are family traditions for trimming the Christmas tree. Throw in what seems to be ever more busy schedules and the consumer rush from Thanksgiving to Christmas, and how we decorate our trees becomes an interesting story in many homes. Sometimes just purchasing a tree and setting it up are major achievements.

At the same time trimming the Christmas tree is often very meaningful, evoking special memories from childhood. Take time to share these stories - while you are picking out a tree, setting it up, retrieving the boxes of decorations from the attic or basement, and while hanging the ornaments and lights. Encourage each family member to share a memory. Often children will share a story you told them in years past!

Bible Readings

*(Have family members choose one of the following passages to read
aloud while trimming the tree.)*

SUGGESTION:

*Read the following passage when you
plug in the lights.*

In the beginning was the Word,
and the Word was with God, and the
Word was God. He was in the beginning with God. All things came into
being through him, and without him
not one thing came into being. In him
was life, and the life was the light of
all people. The light shines in the darkness and the darkness did not overcome it. (John 1:1-5)

SUGGESTION:

*Read the following passage when you
place the star on top of the tree.*

In the time of King Herod, after
Jesus was born in Bethlehem of
Judea, wise men from the East came
to Jerusalem asking, "Where is the
child who is born king of the Jews?
For we have observed his star at its
rising, and have come to pay him
homage ... In Bethlehem of Judea ..."
When they had heard the king, they
set out; and there ahead of them went
the star that they had seen at its rising, until it stopped over the place
where the child was. When they saw
that the star had stopped, they were
overwhelmed with joy. (Matthew 2:1-
2, 5, 9-10).

SUGGESTION:

*Read the following passage when you
begin putting on ornaments and other
trimmings.*

On entering the house, they saw
the child with Mary his mother; and
they knelt down and paid him homage.
Then, opening their treasure chests,
they offered him gifts of gold, frankincense, and myrrh. (Matthew 2:11)

SUGGESTION:

*Read the following passage as you fin-
ish trimming your tree. Then gather
around the tree to sing a Christmas
hymn (Go Tell It on the Mountain, It
Came Upon a Midnight Clear, Joy to
the World).*

In that region there were shepherds living in the fields keeping watch over their flock by night. Then an angel of the Lord stood before them, and the glory of the Lord shone around them, and they were terrified. But the angel said to them, "Do not be afraid; for see; I am bringing good news of a great joy for all the people: to you is born this day in the city of David a Savior, who is the Messiah, the Lord. This will be a sign for you: you will find a child wrapped in bands of cloth and lying in a manger." And suddenly there was with the angel a multitude of the heavenly host, praising God and saying, "Glory to God in the highest heaven, and on earth peace among those whom he favors!" (Luke 2:8-14).

Litany

(Use following while tree-trimming.)

ONE: The scent of pine, the jingle of ornaments, the twinkle of lights, the star shining at the top of the tree bring back memories of Christmases past:

ALL: The joy, the laughter, the fun … time spent together.

ONE: The evergreen pine, the lights, the star also remind us of God's greatest gift:

ALL: Jesus was born the Light of the World, the bright Morning Star, the Alpha and the Omega.

ONE: Jesus, the Light of the World, reminds us that we live in a world where darkness abounds.

ALL: As the lights on our tree bring us joy and delight, let us seek to bring joy to those who suffer, who are lonely, who cannot see the Light.

ONE: Jesus, the bright Morning Star, reminds us that there are those for whom morning means another day of struggle to survive famine or warfare or tyranny.

ALL: As the star in the East led the Magi to Jesus, let us be guiding Lights to bring hope to despairing lives, to bring the good news of salvation.

ONE: Jesus, the Alpha and the Omega, the beginning and the end, reminds us that human life is frail and temporary, and that some feel life is not worth living.

ALL: God has created all things and God will continue to create. We are created in God's image and included in an eternal covenant of love. Let us so live our lives that others find meaning and purpose in their own through Jesus Christ. Amen.

Prayer

(*Gather around the tree, holding hands. Ask someone to lead the prayer or say it in unison.*) Everlasting God, you guide us to the place where Jesus was born with many signs: dreams, stars, angels. But our world, today, pulls us in other directions with neon, Nintendo, and the 'Net.' We are tempted with miracles of technology we can watch or hold in our hands, and are numbed – to the needs of those who so desperately need a sign that somebody – anybody cares. Forgive our weakness and conspicuous consumption.

You guide us to Jesus so that we might learn your Way and in turn show others. Open our eyes to your signs once again. Give us the desire to see the needs of others and to work to meet them. As you gave us your only Son, may we give of our lives and our means, so that others no longer want for even the most basic necessities and can see in us only Jesus as we seek to meet those needs. Make us rays of your light in our darkened world. Amen.

Christmas hymn

(*Conclude your tree-trimming service with a favorite hymn.*)

SUGGESTIONS

- Music adds so much to the time of trimming the Christmas tree. Recordings of traditional carols and new songs in various formats (jazz, big band, etc.) add much and build memories!
- Share some of the ways our culture glosses over Jesus' birth at Christmas. Which ones have found a weakness in you? What can you do to restore a proper focus and meaning to your Christmas celebration?

  Which of your tree trimming traditions point to Jesus' birth, the true meaning of Christmas? Which of them do not? Discuss ways your annual tree trimming could reflect an alternative lifestyle. Write them down and use them.

- Discuss ways you can be the Light of Jesus in another's life. List them, and make plans to do at least one of them. Make sure your plans include interaction with at least one person you do not know.

Service for Sharing Christmas Memories

Heidi Roy

So often we rush through Advent and Christmas and don't take the time to remember what makes the season meaningful. Memories of special celebrations and people are often only flashes of thoughts rushing through our minds as we stand in long lines or unpack decorations.

Set aside some time to gather as a family or small group to acknowledge and share your memories. Ask each person to bring a special Christmas "something," such as a favorite decoration, a photo of Christmas past, a reading, etc. Also gather and bring all of the Christmas cards you received so far this season.

Bible Reading

Luke 2:1-14 *(see page 154-155).*

Litany

(Choose someone to read this aloud or ask each person to read one line.) We gather together to remember what makes Christmas special. For this time, we put aside our thoughts of gift lists and decorating, baking and shopping. We remember the Christ Child and what his birth means to us and our world. *(A few minutes of silence)*

We remember those Christ came to serve, the hungry, the thirsty, the sick, the imprisoned. We remember our family and friends, many of whom we see only during holidays like this. Here and now, we make a commitment to take time during these busy weeks to touch the lives of people as Jesus did in his living and as he continues to do today.

SHARING

One at a time, have each person talk about the photo, decoration, etc. that s/he brought. As the person is sharing, pass the item around so that everyone can see it close up.

Now pass around the stack of Christmas cards you have received. Have each person choose one card and read it aloud. Tell who it is from. Who is the person(s) to you? Share a fond memory of the person. Finally, ask each person to share one thing that made last Christmas meaningful.

SINGING

Sing a favorite carol.

Prayer

(Form a circle and hold hands. Ask someone to lead the group in the following prayer.) O Gracious God, as we make our way through this frantic time of year, help us to remember that Jesus came to bring peace. Though often overshadowed by the "things" of Christmas, that peacefulness is there for us to know and to share. Let us remember that people, not material things, make the season special. Guide us as we reach out to the people around us with the message of Christmas. Amen.

SUGGESTIONS FOR THE WEEKS AHEAD

- Choose some photos of past Christmas celebrations to display during this season. Place them in a prominent place so that you are continually reminded of special people and times.
- Set up a crèche to remind you that Jesus' humble birth is the reason we celebrate.
- Consider setting aside some time each day to meditate on the meaning of Christmas.
- Phone someone you wouldn't normally call. Or make an unexpected visit.
- Consider using money normally spent on Christmas gifts to travel to see family or friends. Talk with others about this idea.
- Volunteer in a local soup kitchen or shelter. Get to know the people.

• During the week after Christmas, write down your thoughts on what made this season special. Put them away to read during the next Christmas season.

A Service for Closing the Season

Kathleen Connolly

At family ritual workshops, people talk about the letdown after Christmas. The turkey's gone. How painful it is to take the tree down, a job which usually falls to the mother in the house. As Director for Christian Life, Kathleen Connolly has initiated an Epiphany Party that includes a Home Mass.

"We've done it for five or six years," Kathleen says. We've gotten good response. This party is not crammed in with Christmas. It falls far enough after Christmas that it is a quieter celebration."

Invitations are sent to friends and members of St. Bridget's Club, an organization open to all at St. Margaret Mary Parish. It includes families of all descriptions – young married, adult singles, religious people. (St. Bridget is the patron saint of hospitality.) Its purpose is to have something social, service-oriented, and spiritual each month. The service project for January is St. Anthony House; the social is the party; and the spiritual is the Home Mass.

The attendees bring items to donate, usually clothing and children's toys, which are given to the homeless shelter and families of migrant workers at St. Anthony House.

The party has evolved. Some 20 families in the church group and their friends come to a potluck supper and home mass, which includes a service of prayers, a period of reflection and a time for reconciliation.

"We are not encouraged to sing Christmas songs before Christmas (during Advent). So, on this Epiphany night, guitar-accompanied music consists of traditional Christmas songs to say good-bye to Christmas and hello to Epiphany."

Service

LEADER

Sometimes we're short with each other at Christmas. We may be disappointed. There are so many expectations at Christmas. In Jesus' name we can now let go of those things and forgive each other when we've been short or jealous. Reflect back on this past Christmas. Share your thoughts. Think of the Bread of Communion. How were you fed and nourished this Season? Where were you famished? *(Pause for response or solicit response.)*

LEADER

How would we like next Christmas to be different, better, more meaningful? *(Pause for response. Leader takes notes which will be kept in a safe place until next fall.)*

LEADER

Join hands to pray. "Everliving and loving God, thank you for the chance to celebrate Jesus' birthday. Forgive us our shortcomings, our envy, our greed. Help us to celebrate even more responsibly throughout this new year. In Jesus' name, Amen."

(Read the Reflection for Epiphany. The group proceeds to take the tree down in home or church. The donated items are collected for distribution.)

Contributors to Part 2 – Celebrate

Let's Go to Bethlehem

MICHAEL CROSBY
is a member of the Midwest Province of the Capuchin Franciscans and a nationally-known speaker and writer. His works include Spirituality of the Beatitudes: Matthew's Challenge to First World Christians; The Seven Last Words; and The Dysfunctional Church. He also serves on the Board of Directors of Alternatives and Editorial Committee.

MARY FOULKE
is Protestant Chaplain at Wellesley College, Cambridge, MA, and a member of Alternatives' Board of Directors.

MICHELLE MCKINNON BUCKLES
focuses on evangelism and membership care as Associate Pastor at First United Methodust Church, Lawrenceville, Georgia.

Reflections on the Gospel Texts

SISTER JOAN CHITTISTER, O.S.B.
Is prioress of The Benedictine Sisters in Erie, Pennsylvania and a member of Sojourners' editorial board.

KAREN GREENWALDT
Former member of Alternatives' Board of Directors, is a clergy member of the Central Texas Conference of the United Methodist Church. She serves as Associate General Secretary of the Discipleship Ministries Unit on the General Board of Discipleship.

Christmas Reflections

TOM SINE

An Episcopalian layman, works in the areas of futures research and planning with major denominations. He is also the director of Mustard Seed Associates. A prolific writer, Tom has written many articles and books, including *Live It Up: How to Create a Life You Can Love* (Herald Press, 1993) and *Cease Fire: Searching for Sanity in America's Culture Wars* (Eerdmans, 1995).

ASHLEY NEDEAU-OWEN

Is Alternatives' Business Manager.

RICK HOFFARTH

Serves as pastor of Locust Presbyterian Church, Locust, North Carolina.

HEIDI ROY

Olive Branch, Mississippi, served on Alternatives' staff for over seven years.

KATHLEEN CONNOLLY

A Roman Catholic living in Orlando, Florida, is a former member of the Board of Directors of Alternatives and is an experienced workshop leader on voluntary simplicity.